MERMAID

CRAFTS

MERMAID CRAFTS

25 MAGICAL PROJECTS FOR DEEP SEA FUN

Isabel Urbina Gallego

Racehorse Publishing

Racehorse Publishing books may be purchased in bulk at special discounts for sales promotion, corporate gifts, fund-raising, or educational purposes. Special editions can also be created to specifications. For details, contact the Special Sales Department, Skyhorse Publishing, 307 West 36th Street, 11th Floor, New York, NY 10018 or info@skyhorsepublishing.com.

Racehorse Publishing™ is a pending trademark of Skyhorse Publishing, Inc.®, a Delaware corporation.

Visit our website at www.skyhorsepublishing.com.

10 9 8 7 6 5 4 3 2 1

Library of Congress Cataloging-in-Publication Data

Names: Gallego, Isabel Urbina, author.
Title: Mermaid crafts: 25 magical projects for deep sea fun / Isabel Urbina Gallego.
Description: New York: Racehorse Publishing, [2019] | Includes bibliographical references and index.
Identifiers: LCCN 2019002476 (print) | LCCN 2019003055 (ebook) | ISBN 9781631584190 (Ebook) | ISBN 9781631584114 (print: alk. paper)
Subjects: LCSH: Handicraft. | Mermaids in art.
Classification: LCC TT160 (ebook) | LCC TT160 .G24 2019 (print) | DDC 745.5—dc23
LC record available at https://lccn.loc.gov/2019002476

Cover design by Mona Lin
Cover photographs by Isabel Urbina Gallego

Print ISBN: 978-1-63158-411-4
Ebook ISBN: 978-1-63158-419-0

Printed in China

CONTENTS

Safety Information

- It is recommended to always take safety precautions when performing manual tasks and activities. Always follow the directions labels and supplies used.

- Always use age judgment and do not allow children under the age of 3 to participate with ingredients or small supplies that may pose a choking hazard.

- It is recommended that all activities and crafts be carried out only under the supervision of an adult.

- Adults should handle any chemical product or sharp tools.

INTRODUCTION

Get ready for an adventure under the sea!

First of all, let me introduce myself—my name is Isa and I am a passionate lover of crafts. I love everything artistic and handmade, and every week I upload videos with tutorials of handcrafts to my YouTube channels. If you want to visit me there, you can find my channels as Isa's World (in English) and El Mundo de Isa (in Spanish).

I have always been mesmerized with the mermaid world; these mythological beings transport us to a universe of underwater fantasy where the day goes by in constant fun.

This book brings us closer to the fantastic underwater universe where mermaids and their aquatic friends live, with dozens of entertaining craft projects. Create treasure chests, jewels worthy of a mermaid princess, fun marine characters, and even your own mermaid doll made with felt cloth.

It doesn't matter if you are a beginner or if you are already a pro crafter. This book is designed for everyone to enjoy their beautiful projects. Each craft comes with its list of materials, templates, detailed instructions, and many pictures for mermaid lovers to immerse their creativity in the coral background. Do you dare to swim with these beautiful creatures?

TREASURE CHEST

*A chest full of treasures rescued from the bottom
of the sea by the mermaids.*

Wouldn't you love to find a chest full of treasures? Who hasn't imagined discovering under the sand of the beach an old chest with valuable objects from a ship of centuries ago . . . Surely in some remote place of the ocean, there are mermaids that recover these chests full of coins and jewels, and now we can make our own.

Difficulty: difficult
Time required: around 5 hours of work + drying time.

Supplies:

* 5mm thick cardboard
* White glue
* Water
* Masking tape
* Newspaper scraps
* Acrylic paints (I use DecoArt Americana)—colors I used: Snow White DA01, Aqua Sky DA333-3, Primary Yellow DA201-3
* Fine sand
* Paintbrushes
* Scissors
* Closure clasp for boxes
* Superglue
* To decorate: Moss, shells, rope or twine, beads, rhinestones, anything extra you'd like

Instructions:

The first step is to prepare your cardboard—this will be the base material to make this treasure chest. I recommend using double-wave (corrugated) cardboard, as this is thicker and more resistant and will be perfect for our craft. As a general rule, double-channel cardboard has a thickness of approximately 5mm.

In this image, you can see some of the pieces of cardboard you need with the corresponding measurements. To cut straight out, you can use a box cutter—ask an adult for help with this!

A pieces correspond to the front and back of the chest.

B piece corresponds to the base of the chest.

C pieces correspond to the sides.

D and **E** pieces correspond to the lid of the chest.

Measurements:

A: 16cm × 10cm

B: 15cm × 10cm

C: 10cm × 10cm

D: 16cm × 3cm

E: 10cm × 3cm in the straight zone and 4cm in the top of the curve

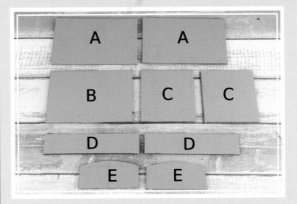

The chest is divided into 2 main pieces—the lid and the box. To make the box, we will use pieces A, B, and C. This is as simple as gluing the pieces together. This glue is slow drying, so you can hold the pieces together with masking tape to stay in place while they dry.

To form the lid, we will use parts D and E. First join the pieces D and E to form the body of the lid.

In the following photo you can see that the piece of upper part is somewhat curved, for this reason I used single-wave cardboard since it is easier to form the rounded shape of the lid—it is important that the waves of the cardboard go in the same direction that you see in the image so they will be able to bend. Take the necessary measures and cut the cardboard and glue it on top with white glue. Now your lid is ready!

We will cover all the edges and corners of the box and the lid with masking tape. This will create a more professional finish to our chest.

To make the chest stronger, we will apply a layer of papier-mâché. This consists of sticking pieces of newspaper across the surface of the chest. To paste it, we will use a mixture of white glue and water.

The paper cutouts that I have used are from an old phone book, this paper is perfect for this craft, and you can also use newspaper scraps.

Create your papier-mâché mixture by combining 70 percent white glue and 30 percent water. Using a paintbrush, apply the glue mixture onto your cardboard chest, completing 1 side at a time. As you go, place the pieces of paper onto the glue, overlapping each other. The papier-mâché should cover the entire chest and lid, inside and outside. Then let it dry overnight.

After several hours (or overnight), your pieces should be dry and resistant—it is now time to join the lid with the box. For this we will use masking tape. Look at the following image to place the pieces correctly, then place a strip of masking tape on the inside of the chest to join them.

If you want to give it extra strength, cover the masking tape with more glue mixture and pieces of newspaper, and let it dry for at least 6 hours.

Now close the chest and place another strip of masking tape along the back of your closed box, covering the space between the lid and the box.

Cool! The hardest part is finished, now comes the fun, which is to paint and decorate. Go for it!

Now we will use acrylic paints! First, apply 2 layers of white paint across the entire chest. Let the paint dry between layers.

As you know, we are making a treasure chest that has spent centuries at the bottom of the sea, so we must give it a worn look. To achieve this, we will apply a painting technique called dry brush. Dip the brush in turquoise paint and blot the excess onto a paper towel. We want the brush to make irregular strokes with just a bit of paint, not too much. Apply these quick brushstrokes all over the chest, you will see that it begins to take on a very beautiful worn look.

On the lower part of the chest we will use yellow paint, using the same dry brush technique.

Once you've done both the blue and yellow portions, we will cover the bottom of the chest with sand. On top of the yellow portion, add a thin layer of glue, and sprinkle your fine beach sand and let it dry. It will stay stuck in the areas where there is glue, and once it's dry you can gently shake the chest so excess sand falls off and the blue area is clear.

And now everything depends on your creativity! You can glue shells, moss, plastic beads, and anything else you like so that your new chest has the desired look. Use superglue to paste all the ornaments.

As a final touch, we will place a nice metal lock that you can get in craft stores. First adhere this with superglue, and then insert small screws to make sure it stays in place.

I love the result of this craft—it is totally realistic and you can save all your treasures here. Or, if you're having a mermaid-themed party, you can fill it with chocolate coins and everyone will be surprised!

Mermaid candy machine

Mermaids loooove sweets!

When I was a young girl, I remember those machines at the front of stores that you had to put a coin, turn a crank, and 2 huge gumballs came out. I still remember the distinct taste—and also how difficult it was to turn the crank as a little kid!

Inspired by those old chewing gum machines, we will make ours with the colors of the sirens, because surely the sirens are as sweet as can be.

Difficulty: easy
Time required: about 1 hour of work + the drying time.

Supplies:

* 1 terra-cotta pot with corresponding dish
* 1 small round fishbowl tank, or a small bowl
* 1 small wooden ball
* High strength universal use glue
* Silk paper
* Masking tape
* Acrylic paints (I used DecoArt Americana in these colors: Bahama Blue DA255-3, Royal Fuchsia DA151-3 , Baby Pink DAO31-3, Snow White DA01, Lilac Meadow DA367-3, Calypso Blue DA234-3, Royal Purple DA150-3)
* Gloss Varnish DuraClear DecoArt Americana DS19
* Pencil
* Paintbrush
* Tissue paper, parchment paper, or another traceable paper

Instructions:

You can find a small terra-cotta pot with a draining plate at any craft or garden store. You can choose the size you want—I found a small size because I want to display this candy machine on my desk (so I can eat candy during working hours!). 🍬

Try to consider the sizes of both the terra-cottapot and the fishbowl—the base of the tank should not overlap the base of the pot too much.

Refer to the template on page 159 to choose which phrase you want on your candy machine. The words are mirrored, so when you trace them onto your pot, they will be read correctly!

You can choose between: "be a mermaid" or "mermaid kisses"—when you have decided which phrase you like the most, trace it in pencil lightly onto your tissue paper.

We will start by painting the pot and the plate. I have chosen colors that remind me of mermaids and the sea, like turquoise, lilac, purple, pink, and magenta. I will combine these colors to create a fun and harmonious contrast, so I decided to paint the pot purple and the plate turquoise. Paint the small wooden ball the same color as your pot. Let it dry and if necessary, apply a second coat of paint.

To transfer the phrase to your pot, turn your (now dry) pot upside down, and place the tissue paper over the pot, so that the pencil marks are in contact with the pot. Add a few bits of masking tape to hold it in place.

Now go over the letters again in pencil so that the words appear lightly on the pot. Then carefully remove the paper and you are ready for the next step.

Then let this dry completely before moving on to the next step.

It's time to color! Use colors that contrast with your background color, so the letters will be easy to read and the result will be brighter.

Use a fine brush to trace the contours since it will allow you to be more precise. You can even outline your letters, if you dare!

If, by mistake, you paint outside the drawing lines, do not worry, let the paint dry and then correct by painting again with the background color.

Once your mermaid phrase is dried, apply 2 coats of varnish to protect the paint and give a very glamorous, bright touch. You must let the varnish dry between layers. Follow the manufacturer's instructions to know the drying times.

Finally, glue your wooden ball to the back of the terra-cotta plate, right in the center. Glue the base of your fishbowl to the bottom of the pot. A universal superglue should be used for the ceramics and glass. Allow these to fully dry before adding candy!

*Now fill your machine with your favorite sweets,
and add your lid as the final touch!*

Mermaid Animal Pens

Is there anything more adorable than a kawaii animal?

Okay, I consider myself a fan of all things kawaii—I love how adorable the kawaii-style animals look, with their tender little faces and flushed cheeks. And what I like the most is that in the kawaii world, imagination has no limits; an animal can be both a mermaid and an ice cream at the same time! Isn't it fascinating that anything is possible? So for this craft I have decided to mix the world of sirens with the kawaii world, with these little mermaid animals that are really fun pens. Aren't they the perfect combination?

Difficulty: medium
Time required: around 2 hours of work + drying time.

Supplies:

- ⭐ 1 pen (per each character)
- ⭐ Jumping Clay (Colors: brown, pink, white, cream, turquoise, red, and black)
- ⭐ Acrylic paints (I used DecoArt Americana in Snow White DA01 and Dark Chocolate DAO65-3)
- ⭐ Gloss Varnish DuraClear DecoArt Americana DS19
- ⭐ Roller to stretch out the clay
- ⭐ Scissors
- ⭐ Star-shaped cake decorating tip
- ⭐ Paintbrush
- ⭐ Ruler
- ⭐ Tissue paper, parchment paper, or another traceable paper

Instructions:

Use a sheet of paper to trace the bear or monkey from the template on page 160, whichever you like the most. I have chosen to show you step-by-step with the monkey-mermaid.

Once you have traced the template, it is time to make the doll. Take a bit of brown clay and roll it out thin so it's pliable. Form it on top of the area that corresponds to the body and tail of the mermaid.

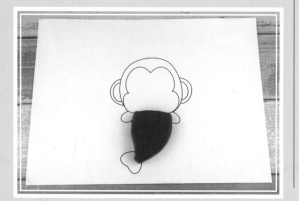

The next step is to situate the pen along the entire body. As you will see in the following image, I have inserted it diagonally to make sure that the pen fits into the template.

Leave this piece aside and move on to the next step.

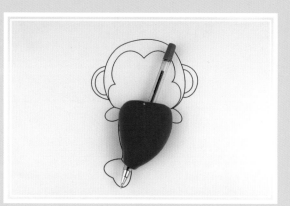

Take a small ball of brown clay and flatten it slightly, adjusting to the area of the head. Make sure that the thickness of the head is the same as the thickness of the body so that everything will fit together.

It is time to join both pieces, so hold the body and pen with one hand, and use your other to carefully secure the head piece onto the pen above the body. Keep in mind that the pen should be in a somewhat inclined position, so the pen should penetrate the head diagonally (refer to the picture to see what I mean).

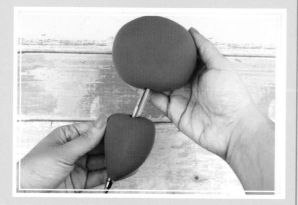

With the help of the template we will also make the ears and arms. Then attach an ear to each side of the head, and secure the arms right between the head and the body. The clay is flexible, so you should be able to attach these without needing glue—though you must also be careful, because once attached it cannot be separated.

To make the face of our monkey-mermaid, cut out that part of the template to use it as a mold.

Use a bit of cream-colored Jumping Clay and roll it out to a sheet about 3 millimeters thick.

Then place the template on the clay and cut the excess dough with a modeling tool that has a sharp edge (you can also do it with a scissor).

Remove the paper template and review the edges of the resulting monkey face shape with your fingertips to smooth out any imperfections. Then place the face on the center of your monkey head.

The base of your doll is already done! Now let's decorate.

As I told you at the beginning of this project, this *kawaii* character that we are creating is not only a monkey-mermaid, but is also an ice cream—so now we are going to shape out his waffle cone tail.

Take the turquoise Jumping Clay and stretch it with the help of the roller. You should have a sheet about 3 millimeters thick.

Use a ruler to form a crisscross shape like the one you see in the next image. Press the ruler lightly into the clay to form diagonal lines in one direction, then do the same in the opposite direction—this is your cone pattern.

Now gently place the waffle pattern around the body of the monkey, leaving space just below the arms (place it at the waist of your monkey-mermaid). Make sure it connects on the back of the doll, so it looks complete.

On the lower part, adjust the the clay so the tip of your pen is not blocked. That way you can refill it with new ink when the pen no longer writes.

To decorate the top of the head, I also made a shape that mimics strawberry syrup with pink Jumping Clay. Roll up your newly created white star-shaped clay to look like whipped cream, and place it on top of the monkey's head.

For the next step, you will need to use the star-shaped pastry bag nozzle.

Little by little, push white clay through the wide part of the decorating tip, so it comes out with a star shape (like a churro). Push enough clay through that you have about a 10cm strand.

To complete the decoration of the head, roll a tiny ball of red clay and thin green stem—the cherry on top!

We are almost finished! Using the same method of rolling tiny balls and flattening them, making 2 small eyes and a nose with black clay, 2 spots of pink cheek blush, and a small pacifier.

I have also added a strawberry syrup–style waistband onto the tail.

And with acrylic paints, give him a pair of brown eyebrows and a few points of light in the eyes with white paint.

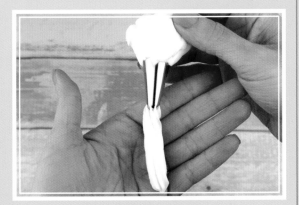

After that 6 hours, you can already nail the tip of the pen and let it dry for another 24 hours in that position. You should not use the pen until the Jumping Clay is completely dry, otherwise it will deform all the work, so be patient and let it dry.

To finish, refer to the template to make a kind of heart shape out of clay, which will be the lid of the pen. It is very important that you let this dry about 6 hours before introducing the tip of the ballpoint pen, so that the pink clay does not stick to the turquoise tail.

With this basic template, you can make any animal that you can think of! Try to make the bear-mermaid next, using only my photo and the monkey's instructions. Can you think of more?

GLOBE MERMAID QUOTE

There's a million fish in the sea, but I'm a mermaid!

I love this phrase: "There's a million fish in the sea, but I'm a mermaid." It means that each of us is a unique being, with distinctive qualities that make each of us special, and we ought to value ourselves and our differences because we are irreplaceable!

I like to have these uplifting and motivating words around to remind us that we are unique and that we can achieve everything we set out to. This inspirational globe makes a beautiful decorative object.

Difficulty: medium
Time required: around 2 hours of work + drying time.

Supplies:

* ⭐ 1 globe
* ⭐ Acrylic paints (I used DecoArt Americana in: Extreme Sheen 24K gold DPM04-30, Aqua Sky DA333-3, Black DAO67-3, Baby Pink DAO31-3, Peony Pink DA215-3, Primary Yellow DA201-3, Holly Green DAO48-3, Irish Moss DA312-3)
* ⭐ Ultra-matte Varnish DuraClear DecoArt Americana DS124-9
* ⭐ Tissue paper, parchment paper, or another traceable paper
* ⭐ Masking tape
* ⭐ Pencil
* ⭐ Scissors
* ⭐ Paintbrush

Instructions:

Choose a globe that can be dismantled easy enough; this will be necessary to separate the foot of the sphere to work more comfortably. It is usually easy to separate these 2 pieces, just open the top clasp a bit and they should separate easily.

The next step is to remove the paper where the map of the earth is printed. I was surprised that it was so easy to remove—the map was not completely stuck to the globe, which saved me a lot of work. It is of course possible that your map will be more difficult to take off. If that's the case, you can put the sphere in hot water for a few minutes to peel off the paper, and then dry it with a towel.

To paint the ball of the globe more comfortably, I have inserted a wooden stick through the holes in the sphere, which holds it in place and you can paint it without getting your hands too messy. I have chosen a blue color that reminds us of the blue of the sky.

Let it dry at least 2 hours.

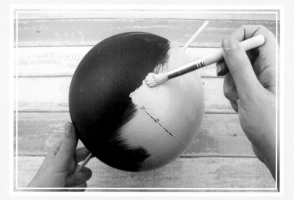

The base, where the sphere is inserted, I painted with gold paint that has metallic effect.

To obtain full coverage, I recommend that you apply 2 coats of paint to both the globe and base, letting them dry at least 2 hours between layers.

When both the base and the sphere are dry, you can reconnect them.

Refer to the template on page 161 to find the phrase that I have prepared in a popular calligraphy style.

As you can see, the phrase is written in mirror mode, so that when you transfer it to the balloon, it is read correctly.

Trace the phrase with pencil onto tissue or parchment paper. Then cut out each line of words and place them on the sphere, trying to fit the words across the entire globe. In order to transfer the pencil graphite, you must place it so that the pencil marks are in contact with the globe's surface.

Lightly tape the tissue paper with masking tape to hold it in place, then lightly press all over the pencil area with a rounded object, like the back of the scissors. This will press the graphite onto the painted globe.

Once you have transferred all the letters, carefully remove the paper.

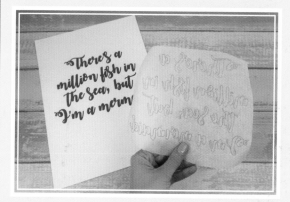

If you would like to in this step, you can re-separate the sphere from the globe to paint it.

Use a fine brush to fill all the letters with black paint. Take all the time you need to do this, to try to stay inside the outline of the letters. If you make a mistake, just let it dry and then correct the imperfections with the sky blue paint we used before.

Finally, paint some simple flowers or other decorations around the quote—just a few strokes of color will keep it simple.

Once your words and flowers are all dry, apply a layer of varnish to protect your paint and let it dry.

You can make this motivational globe to decorate your desk or give it to a friend. Surely it will be an uplifting gift! 😄

CHEST OF DRAWERS

This miniature cabinet will help you organize your belongings.

This is a great and useful craft because it will help us keep our desk or dresser tidy. It is hand painted with simple marine drawings, and will bring a bit of the sea to your room.

We only need cardboard and some other materials to create a small cabinet that will stand out wherever you choose to place it.

Difficulty: medium
Time required: around 5 hours of work + drying time.

Supplies:

- ✰ 5mm thick cardboard
- ✰ White glue
- ✰ Masking tape
- ✰ 3 small wooden balls
- ✰ Acrylic paints (I used DecoArt Americana in: Baby Blue DAO42-3 , Lilac Meadow DA367, Snow White DA01, Shoreline DA365-3, Ocean Blue DA270-3, Bubblegum Pink DA250-3, Cadmium Yellow DAO10-3, Black DAO67-3, Yellow Green DA134-3, Peaches 'n Cream DAO23-3)
- ✰ Gloss Varnish DuraClear DecoArt Americana DS19
- ✰ Pencil
- ✰ Paintbrush
- ✰ Box cutter
- ✰ Black permanent marker

Instructions:

In the following image you can see some of the cardboard pieces you need, they are named with letters so you can easily identify them and the measurements are described below. To cut straight out you can use a box cutter, but if you are young, you should ask an adult for help with this step.

- **A:** the front of the chest.
- **B:** the back of the chest.
- **C:** the upper part of the chest, the drawer floors, and the base.
- **D:** the sides of the chest.

Measurements:

A: total exterior measurement 17cm × 20.5cm (the gaps measure 15.5cm × 6cm) and the width of all the cardboard strips is 0.5cm except the lower strip that is 1cm wide.

- **B:** 17cm × 20.5cm
- **C:** 14cm × 16cm
- **D:** 14cm × 20.5cm

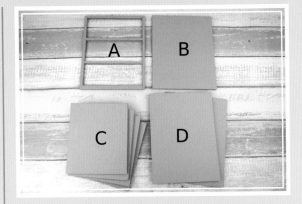

Using white glue to join the pieces, take your "A" piece with the cutouts and attach a D piece to it.

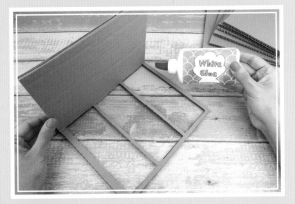

Place this D piece facedown and use white glue to attach 4 evenly spaced C pieces. These should align with the cutouts.

Add another D piece on top of the C's you just added, to form another side of the chest.

Finally glue the B piece to form the back of your chest.

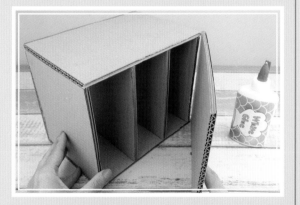

Use masking tape to cover all edges of cardboard, this will make it more stable and also hides the holes in the cardboard.

Now we will make the bottom border of the chest.

Cut 4 strips of cardboard 1cm wide—2 of them must measure 18.5cm long and the other 2 will be 15cm long.

Cover these with masking tape.

Stand your chest upright and draw a line 0.5cm from the bottom edge. This line should be drawn around the entire outline of the base.

Now, following the line you drew, paste on your cardboard strips lined with masking tape.

Phenomenal! The structure is ready, now we will make the drawers.

You must cut more pieces of cardboard. As before, in the next image you will see the pieces of cardboard identified with letters, so it will be easier to understand how you should paste them.

These steps will teach you how to make a drawer, but remember that you need 3 drawers, so you'll need to repeat this process 3 times.

- **E:** base of the drawer.
- **F:** front and rear of the drawer.
- **G:** sides of the drawer.

Measurements:

- **E:** 13.5cm × 14cm
- **F:** 15cm × 5.5cm
- **G:** 13.5cm × 5.5cm

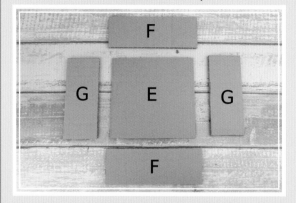

Lay piece E down flat. Glue on both F pieces opposite each other, then glue on both G pieces to connect them.

Repeat this to make 2 more drawers.

Just like earlier, cover all edges of the drawers with masking tape to help stabilize them.

Check that your drawers will fit into the chest properly. On the front of each drawer, glue 1 of your small wooden balls to act as a handle. If you like, you can draw your mark before pasting to ensure each handle will match.

Super! Now we get to color.

We will use acrylic paints for this part. In the list of materials you have the colors that I have used, however, feel free to choose the colors that you like and express your own creativity. But I do advise that you first apply a base layer of white to the entire piece, so that when painting on top, the rest of the colors will really come to life.

I wanted this small chest of drawers to resemble the ocean, so I used different shades of blue to give it that watery look. A little lighter in the central parts and somewhat darker on the ends.

Throughout the lower part, I painted with yellow and ocher colors to simulate the sand of the sea, and I then outlined it with permanent black marker.

With a pencil, draw on some simple marine characters—you can add mermaids and some of their friends, crabs, octopuses, fish, etc. . . . and don't forget to add plenty of bubbles!

Finally, paint in your drawings and outline them with permanent black marker. Let it all dry.

To protect your new craft, also apply a layer of varnish both to the base of the chest and in the drawers. Let the pieces dry separately so that the different parts don't stick together.

You can be proud of your professional creation. It really seems that we have brought home a small piece of the ocean. I love it!

Mermaid Headband

Adorn your hair with this decorative headband directly from the coral bottom.

I love accessories in the hair, ribbons, headbands, clips—they just add such a fun touch. And in my collection of accessories, you'd definitely find a mermaid tiara full of corals and shells! You will have no problem with this quick and easy craft.

Difficulty: easy
Time required: 30 minutes.

Supplies:

- Felt fabric of various colors (try to use colors that remind you of the sea)
- Tissue paper, parchment paper, or another traceable paper
- A plain plastic headband
- Felt-like color markers
- Liquid silicone glue
- Adhesive rhinestones
- Masking tape
- Scissors

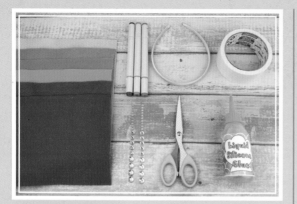

Instructions:

The material I have used here is felt fabric. I recommend using 100 percent wool felt since the details come out better than with synthetic felt.

Page 162 provides you with the shapes. Trace these onto a piece of paper and use tape to adhere the shapes to the felt fabric so it is easier to cut. You can choose any color of felt you like.

Now that you have all the pieces cut out, use markers to add a bit of detail to your corals and shells.

Use liquid silicone glue to add some shiny rhinestones as well!

Finally, you can add all the pieces to your headband, but try to place larger pieces in the back and add smaller ones on top, so they will all be seen clearly.

Use liquid silicone glue to attach your felt pieces, and let it dry at least 3 hours before wearing.

Now you can decorate any hairstyle with this beautiful accessory that reminds us of the world of our beloved mermaids.

This was a simpler craft—are you ready for bigger challenges? Just turn the page and you will find many projects that will challenge your creativity!

Sea Creature Decorated Jars

We'll use recycled jars for this project!

With this project we will convert canning jars into attractive decorations featuring the friends of the mermaids.

These jars can be used for many purposes; I use them to store treats and have them on my desk, so they are decorative and functional. These would also be great to use for a mermaid birthday party.

Difficulty: easy
Time required: around 2 hours of work + drying time.

Supplies:

* Various sized jars, like those used for jelly
* Jumping Clay of various colors
* Scissors
* Roller to stretch the dough
* Modeling tool
* Toothpicks

Instructions:

Start by removing the jar lids, since that's the only piece we really need to decorate.

I used blue Jumping Clay as a base for all the jars, so they all match each other.

Use a rolling pin to stretch the clay and place the lid on top. Jumping Clay is a type of modeling paste that sticks to the contact, so you will not need glue in this project.

Cover the lid with the blue clay and cut off the excess—make sure there is no clay inside the lid so that the jar can then be closed without problems.

Use various colors to make some marine-style decorations. You can make rocks, seaweed, marine corals, pearls, etc. . . . Look at the following image for inspiration to create your decorations.

The first friend of the mermaids that we will create will be the crab.

I chose to decorate with the crab first because according to the classic tale of *The Little Mermaid*, a crab was her faithful companion who advised and accompanied her in all adventures.

Use red Jumping Clay for the body and the black and white colors to make your eyes. This animal is very easy to make, just follow the steps you see in the image to make your crab.

Now place the crab on the lid that we decorated earlier. If the clay on the lid is already somewhat dry the crab will not stay stuck, in this case you can moisten with water or paste it with school glue.

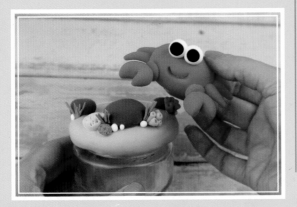

The second friend of the mermaids we'll make will be the octopus.

This is a very fascinating creature—they say octopuses are very intelligent and that they can change the color and texture of their skin to adapt to their environment.

To make our little octopus, I used pink Jumping Clay for the body, yellow for the suction cups, and black and white for the eyes.

Start with making 8 tentacles.

To make the suckers, make small yellow balls, then poke a small hole in each of them with the tip of a toothpick.

Take a small amount of pink clay and squash it flat to use as the base for your tentacles.

Finally, make a pink ball that will be your head and add big eyes with black and white clay.

Place the octopus on a decorated lid. Lay your tentacles across rocks and algae. Now you have an extra friendly face around!

And as the last character to decorate my jars, I had to have a small fish.
There are fish of thousands of colors in the sea, so you can choose any color you like to make this animal.
Look at the following image to see the simple steps and details to follow.

Give her a small smile and place it on your last decorated lid. I have placed it on some gray rocks and it looks like my fish is swimming among seaweed; isn't it adorable?

Express your creativity by making more aquatic animals of your own!

Mermaid Arrow Board

Show off your love of mermaids!

How do you know if you have a mermaid soul? If you enjoy nature, you love the water and the freedom that you feel when you swim in a lake or in the sea, if you believe in the rights of animals, and you feel that there is something magical in your heart . . . then there is a siren inside you. So now, we will create a poster to decorate the entrance to your room, so everyone will know that a siren lives there.

Difficulty: medium
Time required: around 2 hours of work + drying time.

Supplies:

* 1 piece of cardboard, 40cm × 30cm
* Measuring square
* Pencil
* Masking tape
* Scissors
* Tissue paper, parchment paper, or another traceable paper
* Black foam paper
* 2 plastic craft googly eyes
* Scraps of recycled paper
* White glue
* Water
* Superglue
* Silver-colored nail polish
* Acrylic paints (I used DecoArt Americana Aqua Sky DA333-3)
* Paintbrush

Instructions:

First, prepare your cardboard. You can recycle a box that you have at home. This craft can actually adjust to the size you want, it does not have to be the exact 40cm × 30cm and 5mm thick measurements that I used.

Use a square or ruler to draw an arrow on the cardboard like the one seen in the next image. Then cut it out (if you need help, please ask an adult to help you with this step).

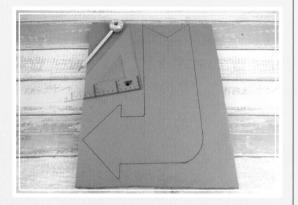

Now that we have the arrow shape cut into the cardboard, cover all of the edges using masking tape, so the sign is more stable and protected.

In a bowl, combine approximately 70 percent white glue with 30 percent water.

You will also need paper scraps, like a recycled phone book or newspaper (these are perfect because the paper is quite thin).

Now use a brush to stick pieces of paper all over the cardboard until it is covered. Be careful to smooth out the paper and try not to leave any lumps, so there is a smooth surface when it dries. When you have covered 1 side, let it dry (will take a few hours) and then do the same with the other side.

When the glue has dried, you will have created a fairly stable surface, so your craft will be resistant and less likely to be damaged over time.

Now is the time to paint. I have chosen the turquoise color, since it reminds me of the sirens and the underwater world.

While the paint dries, we will create the letters of the poster. Follow the template on page 163 for the words MERMAIDS PLEASE ENTER; you'll need to trace this in pencil onto your tracing paper.

Adhere your traced words onto black foam paper. Do this by lightly taping your traced words to the black page so that the pencil graphite is in contact with the foam paper. Now press the pencil area with some rounded object (I always use the back of the scissors for this) and you will notice that the pencil is transferred to the foam paper. Now it will be very easy to cut out each letter from the foam paper.

It's time to paste the letters on the poster in the form of an arrow—you can use superglue for this.

I also cut some strips of black foam paper, 1cm wide, and I have stuck it all around the arrow to add a border.

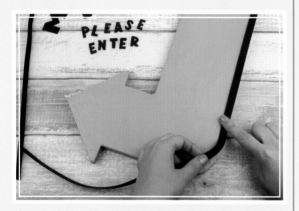

And now I'll show you a trick to make this sign look like metal.

Since this type of arrow sign is usually made of metal, we can make ours look that way too, with some extra details.

First, we need to add "screws" to give realism to the poster. For this you can use plastic googly eyes, which you can find in craft stores. Paint them with black acrylic paint and let them dry. Then stick 1 on each side of the second letter M in "MERMAIDS" in the center of the poster.

Then use a silver-colored metallic nail polish and add brushstrokes to different areas of the poster, but don't paint it completely—you should still see some of the black. This will give you a very realistic worn and metallic look.

Let the polish dry, then your craft will be finished and ready to decorate the entrance to your room.

This decoration will clearly say, Mermaids, please enter!

Mermaid Tail Ring Holder

A beautiful mermaid tail to keep your rings.

I don't usually wear many rings because I always lose them—I'm a little clueless with small things and I never remember where I left them.

But from now on I will always know exactly where they are—with this beautiful mermaid tail of metallic colors.

Difficulty: medium
Time required: around 2 hours of work + drying time.

Supplies:

* Air-hardening modeling clay
* Water
* Acrylic paints (I used DecoArt Americana in: Black DAO67-3, Dazzling Metallics Peacock Pearl DA314-3, Extreme Sheen Pink Tourmaline DPM15-30, Metallic Lustre Gold Rush ML02C-28)
* Roller to stretch the clay
* 10cm diameter cookie cutter
* Small bowl
* Wire
* White glue

Instructions:

To make this craft we will use air-hardening modeling clay, which is a type of clay that does not require baking and is very easy to model. However, this could stain your hands and the table, so make sure to use something to protect the surface, like a plastic sheet or a plastic tablecloth.

This clay is usually a little dry when you open the package, so you should keep a bowl of water nearby to moisten it from time to time. Your hands should also be damp so that the clay does not stick.

We will start by making the dish where the mermaid tail will be stuck.

Roll out some clay to approximately 4mm thick. Then use a cookie cutter to mark a round shape—this should have a diameter of approximately 10cm. I chose a flower-shaped cutter.

In order to give the dish a concave shape, let it dry inside a bowl, so it will adapt to the shape of the bowl. This clay takes about 6 to 12 hours to dry depending on the humidity of the environment.

With another bit of clay, make a cone shape, which will be the mermaid tail. The size is your choice, but note that it must fit inside the small dish you made earlier. Mine is about 4cm wide at the base and 10cm tall.

Use your wire to make a "Y" shape as shown in the following image; this will be the shape of the mermaid tail.

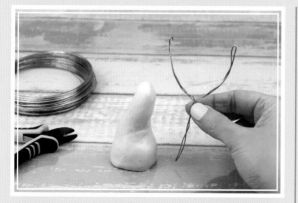

Insert the wire through the narrow part of the cone. You can give the cone a somewhat curved shape so it looks like the tail has some movement.

This wire will also serve to keep the mermaid tail erect while drying.

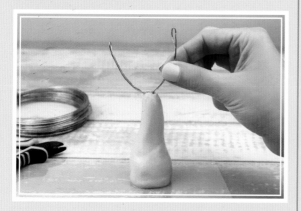

With a wire eyelet, make marks all over the cone to simulate the scales of the mermaid tail, then let it dry for 2 hours.

The next step is to make the fins.

Stretch out a little clay and lay the wire fins over it. Cut the excess clay around the wire, leaving a little extra margin for modeling around the wire. With your hands, mold the clay to cover the wire and shape it into mermaid fins.

You can make some marks to make it more realistic.

Let it dry overnight.

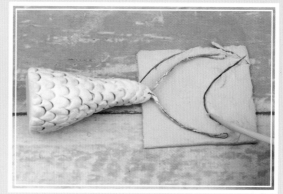

Once ready, carefully remove the dish you had drying inside the bowl. It may be a little stuck at first, but should detach easily.

At this point the mermaid tail should also be completely dry. Glue the 2 pieces together as shown, and let this dry.

Great! Now it is time to paint!

This time, our craft will have a metallic appearance, which will remind us of a mermaid submerging in the sea with its tail illuminated by the light of the moon (mermaids are very poetic!).

Paint the entire craft black and let it dry. This will ensure that you see a black background between the scales where the metallic paint doesn't cover.

Then use the turquoise and fuchsia metallic colors to paint the tail of the mermaid and the plate.

When it is dry, finish with the golden-colored luster to paint the bottom of the plate and also give it some extra touches by the mermaid tail.

I love the metallic aspect of this mermaid tail ring holder, and I'll never lose my rings again. 😊

Mermaid Felt Doll

Don't you want to make this little mermaid doll you can take everywhere?

Here I will teach you how to make your own mermaid doll. The best part is that it is totally customizable—you can choose the color of the hair, the skin, the tail, the accessories, etc. . . . You can even make several and collect them for more fun.

Any type of felt could be used to make this project, however I personally recommend using 100 percent wool felt as it is much easier to sew and the final product of the work shows the details much better. It will also be kept in better condition over the years.

Difficulty: difficult
Required time: around 8 hours.

Supplies:

- ⭐ Tissue paper, parchment paper, or another traceable paper
- ⭐ Felt fabric colors: turquoise, fuchsia, leather, pink, and yellow
- ⭐ 1 sheet of bond paper
- ⭐ Cushion filling
- ⭐ 1 pipe cleaner
- ⭐ Red pencil and normal pencil
- ⭐ Masking tape
- ⭐ Threads of the same colors as the felt as well as black thread
- ⭐ Wool to make hair
- ⭐ Scissors
- ⭐ Needle
- ⭐ Liquid silicone glue

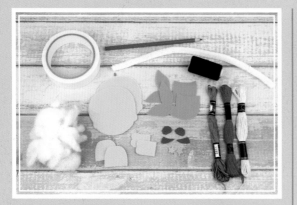

We will do this project by hand with needle and thread. In each step, I've indicated which type of stitch is best to use. To make it easy for you to recognize them, I will briefly explain the types of stitches we are going to use:

Running Stitch: Work from right to left. Bring thread up at 1 then down at 2, up at 3 and down at 4, and continue. The spaces between the stitches can be the same length as the stitches or shorter for a different look.

Instructions:

In the template on page 164, you have all the pieces you need to make this little mermaid. These images are real size, so trace all the pieces on a sheet of paper.

    Cut out each piece of paper individually, and carefully tape the paper to the felt fabric using masking tape.

    Now trim the paper and the felt fabric at the same time to make your felt cutouts. Then discard the paper and, voilà! Your pieces are ready.

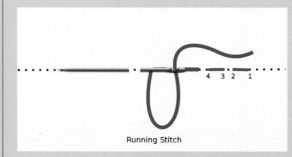

Running Stitch

Back Stitch: Work from right to left. Bring needle up at 1 and back down at 2. Move left and bring needle up at 3, then back down at 1. Continue stitching.

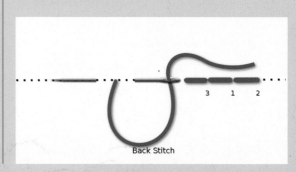

Back Stitch

Overcast Stitch and Appliqué Stitch: Both seams are used to join 2 fabrics.

Overcast Stitch is used to sew 2 fabrics by its edge, and the Appliqué Stitch is used to sew a piece of small cloth over another larger fabric. But they both have the same method. Take the needle from the back of the fabric to the front, making sure to pierce both pieces of fabric to join them. Bring the needle now toward the back through the fabric and go back to the front, continue sewing the seam.

Overcast Stitch

Ladder Stitch: Bring the needle up in A and through the fabric at a short distance from B, keeping the thread hidden under the fabric (light blue lines). Bring the needle to C and through the visible part of the fabric take the needle to D, keeping the thread hidden by the back of the fabric take the needle to E and repeat. Only vertical stitches should be shown on the front of the fabric. The stitches indicated by lines in soft blue color will hide in the base fabric or in the folds of the application. Continue sewing.

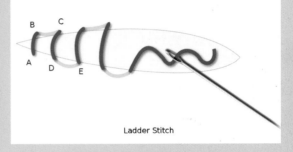

Ladder Stitch

Now let's start making our mermaid doll.

In the following diagram you can see in illustrated way each step that we will do and then you can read the instructions of each step.

Don't worry because this is not as difficult as it may seem, it is much easier when you get down to work.

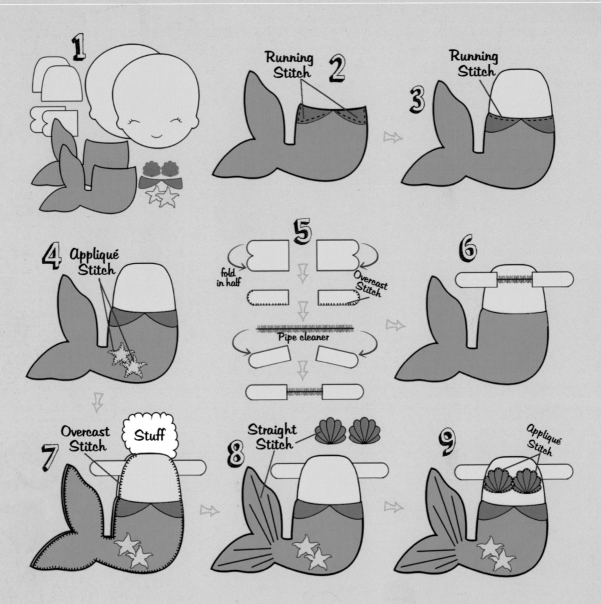

1

2 Running Stitch

3 Running Stitch

4 Appliqué Stitch

5 fold in half   Overcast Stitch   Pipe cleaner

6

7 Overcast Stitch   Stuff

8 Straight Stitch

9 Appliqué Stitch

1. Cut all the felt pieces in their corresponding color. We will need 1 piece for the belt, and 2 pieces each for the body, head, arms, tail, bikini, and 2 pieces of different color for the stars.
2. Attach the fuchsia belt to 1 of the tail pieces using fuchsia thread and Running Stitch.
3. Then take 1 of the skin-colored pieces of the body and place it behind the tail as shown in point 3 of the diagram, sew with fuchsia thread and Running Stitch.
4. To attach the starfish, try to use thread of the same color as the stars and Appliqué Stitch.
5. Now we will form the 2 arms, fold the pieces on themselves and sew with Overcast Stitch, the seam will go on the lower part of the arm.

   Insert a pipe cleaner into 1 of the arms at one end, then cut it down to the size you need to then be hidden inside the body of the wrist. Then insert the other arm through the other end of the pipe cleaner.

6. To form the back, take the second pieces of the body and tail, and join them as you did with the front pieces. Now place the arms at the height of the shoulders and check that the pipe cleaner is the right size.
7. Place on this the front of the doll that you already have ready and join them with Overcast Stitch, you must use thread of similar color to what you are sewing. Don't sew the neck area, and fill with padding. You can help with a pencil to push the filling to all areas of the doll. You must fill enough to make it look bulky.
8. To decorate the tail, make a few lines with white thread and Straight Stitch. Do the same with the 2 pieces of the bikini.
9. Sew the bikini to the body of the doll with fuchsia thread and Appliqué Stitch.

The body of the doll is already finished, in the following diagram you will see the step by step of the head!

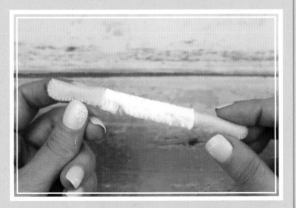

back
stitch

Stuff

Ladder
Stitch

Overcast
Stitch

Don't
sew this

10. Take 1 of the pieces that will form the head and using Back Stitch, sew the eyes with black thread and the mouth with fuchsia.

    You can draw first with a pencil and then sew over the drawn lines, but they must be very soft strokes so that after they are hidden behind the thread.

11. Take the other piece of the head and place it just behind the face. Join them with Overcast Stitch and thread of a color similar to that of the felt, but leave the part of the neck without sewing and then unite the body around that area.

    Before finishing sewing, fill the head with padding and then finish the seam to close the head.

12. Join the head with the body with Ladder Stitch and thread of the same color of the felt. It sews both the front and the back.

To finish, paint some blush marks with red pencil. To decorate the belt, I have stuck a bright plastic adhesive.

This is undoubtedly the most elaborate handicraft of this book, but when you make your first doll you cannot stop! Don't be discouraged, we're almost finished.

It's time to put the hair on this little mermaid—I'm using pink cotton wool, which has a nice soft touch, but any type of wool will work.

Place a pair of pins to mark the area where the doll will have hair.

Then place wool strands over the head of the doll as shown in the image.

Put liquid silicone glue on the back of the head and stick a layer of yarn, then fold back the rest of the yarn, but without sticking it.

Now make a small hole in the top seam of the head, only the size of the nozzle of the liquid silicone glue, and put a tiny bit of glue on the inside of the head. Take a lock made of some strands of wool and insert 1 end through the hole, let the glue dry, and give your mermaid a nice haircut.

You can also put a flower to decorate her hairstyle.

Awesome! You finished your beautiful felt doll, now give it a nice name and . . . make some more friends if you dare. 😍

MERMAID CUP

This mug will surely make you feel like a mermaid first thing in the morning!

A fun way to personalize a cup is to decorate it with polymer clay, you can make beautiful figures with this material.

This time we will decorate with an adorable mermaid—I think this will become your favorite mug to use from now on.

Polymer clay requires baking to harden, so if you're young, ask an adult for help when you get to that step.

Difficulty: medium
Time required: around 1 hour of work + baking time.

Supplies:

★ 1 ceramic cup or mug
★ Colorful polymer clay: fuchsia, light beige, lilac, purple, blue, and white
★ Glue for ceramics
★ Permanent black marker
★ Gloss Varnish DuraClear DecoArt Americana DS19
★ Modeling tools

Instructions:

I like to use polymer clay because it is quite flexible to work with and obtain great results.

This type of clay is available in many colors, and these colors can be mixed together to create new colors and after baking can be painted and varnished.

Because the polymer clay is packed in small bricks, you might think that it is difficult to work with, but after kneading it for a few minutes, it becomes soft and flexible.

We will work directly on the cup to create our mermaid.

Take a small ball of fuchsia clay and place it on the area where the head of the mermaid will go. Flatten it until you get the desired size; this will be the back of the hair.

To make the face, take half a sphere of light beige color and place it just on top of the fuchsia piece.

With your finger, lightly press the area where the eyes and forehead will go, this will help the mermaid cheeks be rounded.

Create a small triangle of light beige clay for the body. Position it just below the face so that the tip of the triangle is in contact with the lower part of the face.

With the lilac color, we will make the mermaid tail and place it just below the body, so they are connected. Look at the following image to see how you should model this part of the mermaid.

With the purple, roll a thin strand to decorate the top of your tail, and also add the tail fins.

Now roll 2 small pieces for a pair of arms and place 1 on each side of the body.

To make shells for the bikini, make 2 small fuchsia balls and use a modeling tool to mark a few stripes to give them the shape of a shell.

Put these shells on the body a little below the shoulder line.

The next step is to make hair. Roll out thin strands of pink color and place them together to form the hair. Wind and curl the ends a little for some extra detail.

Add an ornament on the hair, such as a small lilac star.

I have decorated the cup with circles of the same colors we have used to make the whole mermaid, so is the colors are more harmonious.

Also make a small slit in the mouth—you can do it with your nail or with a modeling tool that has this curved shape.

Then it's time to bake. Please get an adult for this step. Put the cup in the oven and follow the manufacturer's instructions for your baking clay to know how long it needs. In my case, I needed to bake for 30 minutes at 230°F.

When the baking is done, allow the cup to cool completely before continuing.

The clay has been fully baked and hardened on the cup but is not stuck, so if you leverage a bit, it will detach very easily. Remove all pieces of your mermaid from the cup and re-glue them in place using glue suitable for ceramics.

Finally, paint some simple eyes with a fine-tipped permanent marker.

As you can see, I made her eyes closed which is very easy to draw, it's just a couple of curved lines and 3 lines at the end for eyelashes.

To give it a shiny appearance, you can apply a layer of varnish to the mermaid and the circles around it. Let it dry a few hours and it will be ready.

Tip: It is best to wash this by hand with a soft sponge. Do not use it in the microwave or dishwasher.

I want to use this all day long!

Secret Diary

Write your secrets in an old diary that a mermaid
found at the bottom of the sea . . .

The sea keeps many secrets, among them are the mermaids, mysterious beings that few people claim to have seen, and that is part of the sea's charm.

Inspired by this underwater mystery, I created this beautiful journal that imitates an old ship's logbook lost in the bottom of the ocean and that some curious little mermaid rescued to write her own adventures. Do you dare to open it?

Difficulty: difficult
Time required: around 6 hours of work + drying time.

Supplies:

* 60 bond paper sheets, 80gr.
* Liquid silicone glue, white glue, and superglue
* 3 stationery clips
* Pressed gray cardboard, 3mm thick
* Blue and white foam paper
* Acrylic paints (I used DecoArt Americana in: Ultra Blue Deep DA100-3, Sweet Mint DA317-3, Purple Pizzazz DA302-3, Sapphire DPM17-30, Snow White DA01, Citron Green DA235-3, Bronze DPM06-30, Lamp (Ebony) Black DAO67-3)
* Gloss Varnish DuraClear DecoArt Americana DS19
* Double-sided adhesive tape
* Metallic cardboard of golden color
* White Jumping Clay
* Blue glitter powder
* Tissue paper, parchment paper, or another traceable paper
* Sequins or rhinestones
* Plastic netting (I have recycled a piece of a vegetable packing bag)
* Pencil, scissors, brush, and sponge to paint
* Hook and loop

Instructions:

We will start by creating the inside sheets of the journal. You need 60 sheets of 80gr bond paper to get a diary like mine.

Fold each piece of paper in half—you must be exact in this step since it is important that all leaves are even, so take your time to do it carefully.

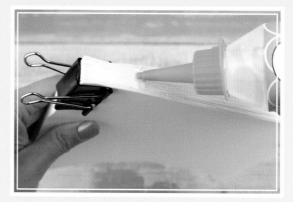

Now that you have all the sheets folded in half, align them precisely, so all the folds go in the same place. When you have it, hold it in place with stationery clips. The area where you have the folds of the leaves should be free to apply the glue.

Binding the pages is quite simple and and effective, it is about applying liquid silicone glue on the sheets so that they stay together like a book. This type of glue is still flexible when dry, so it is ideal to open and close the journal without pages falling off. Apply a generous layer of this glue and let it dry completely, which will take a few hours.

Meanwhile, we are going to create the cover. Cut a piece of blue foam paper that measures 35cm × 22cm. You also need 2 pieces of pressed gray cardboard of 21.5cm × 15cm and a piece of 21.5cm × 2cm.

Paste the cardboard pieces onto the foam paper using liquid silicone glue. Look at the following image and you will see that I have left a small gap between the cardboard pieces of approximately 4mm. This is the hinge area and it is important so that later the newspaper can be closed without problems.

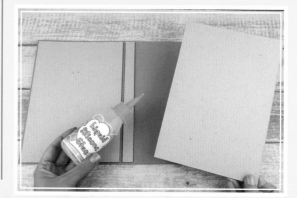

It is time to paint! In this case we are going to paint the foam paper to create a background that imitates the ocean.

I have tried to create an aged effect using a sponge to paint, this consists of applying the paint in light touches and overlapping some colors with others, trying to blur the areas where we change color. We want this to be similar to the colors we can find on the ocean floor, so I have used blue, purple, and mint colors. I also used a metallic blue color to give a brighter touch in some areas.

To make the paint blend easily, you can moisten the sponge with a little water and it will be easier to create the degraded effects.

When the paint has dried, turn it over and we will work in the area where the cardboard is.

Look at the following image. You will notice that I have painted the outer parts of the cardboard with navy blue, this is so that the gray color of the cardboard is not seen when the journal is finished.

The inside pages of our diary will be made of gold-colored metallic cardboard. To stick them we will use double-sided adhesive tape. See how I placed the tape in the picture, and do this for both the right and left side.

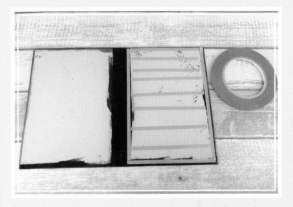

Cut 2 sheets of gilded cardboard of 30cm × 21.5cm, 1 for each of the back pages of the journal.

Take 1 of the sheets and fold it in half, leaving the golden part inwards, then place it on the double sided tape that you put on the right side of the diary, the folded area should be on the inside of the diary. Do the same with the other sheet of cardboard, this time sticking it on the left side.

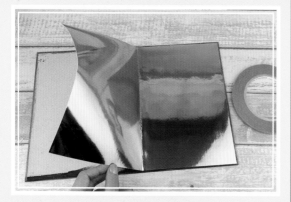

At this point , the sheets of the diary must be completely dry. It is time to place them in the central part of the cover that we have created previously.

Use double-sided tape to glue the pages between the gold cards. Make sure they are centered.

Great! We have completed the most laborious part, now we can have fun decorating the diary.

We are going to make an octopus that emerges from the bottom of the sea and traps the newspaper with its tentacles. This is simpler than it sounds.

Take a little white Jumping Clay. Make a ball of less than 1 inch in diameter. Roll it to reduce the thickness, so there is a thick tip and a thin tip.

Now make tiny balls of Jumping Clay, no larger than the size of grains of rice, and with the help of something sharp, place them along the entire tentacle.

Now give the tentacle a bit of a curve and let it dry for a few hours, then you can paint it in whichever colors you like.

Repeat this for 3 more tentacles.

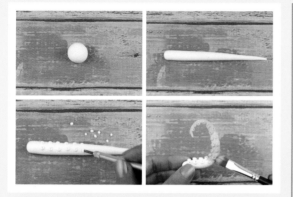

When you have your 4 tentacles ready and the paint has dried, it is time to join them.

Take a ball of Jumping Clay and flatten it at the base, now attach the tentacles through the widest part of these.

Then apply white glue to the clay where you have added the tentacles and sprinkle some blue glitter powder over it. When the glue has dried, shake the tentacles to remove excess glitter.

Set this aside for later.

See the template on page 165 for the figures you must trace with pencil on parchment or tissue paper. These figures should be made in white foam paper (or any light color).

Once you've traced the various items, place the baking paper on the foam by putting the graphite of the pencil in contact with the foam paper. Use something rounded (like the back of scissors) to go over the pencil area. This will cause the graphite to transfer to the foam paper and make it easier to cut out the figures.

Once you have all the pieces cut out in foam paper, paint them with bronze metallic paint and let them dry.

Also get a piece of plastic net—mine is a piece of a net bag from the grocery store, that is sometimes used for things like potatoes or oranges. Paint this with bronze metallic paint and let it dry.

With foam paper, make 2 strips of 30cm × 1.5cm and other 2 strips of 19cm × 1.5cm. Also cut a wider strip of 7cm × 4cm. Paint all these strips with bronze metallic paint and let them dry.

On the 7cm × 4cm wide strip, glue the piece you previously made with a lock with superglue. You can make a pair of Jumping Clay screws to give it more realism. Look at the following image to see how.

In the image that appears below, you can see how you should place the piece that simulates the lock of the diary, if you look, you will see that I have pasted it on the back cover as centered as possible. On top of this I have pasted the long strips that we made in the previous step to frame the entire diary.

For the front of the diary you must paste the rest of the decorations that we had created. Stick the gears, the little net, the sea horses, the octopus, etc. . . . you can also add sequins to give a touch of sparkle. To paste all these pieces, use small amounts of superglue.

Isn't this diary incredible? It really looks like something out of a fantasy tale of mermaids and sailors. Now you can start writing your secrets and adventures in this beautiful diary made by yourself!

As a closure, put a piece of hook and loop through the inside of the lock, so it will look like you need a key to open the diary.

Finally, you can protect the paint with a thin layer of varnish.

MERMAID CAT PLUSH WITH SOCKS

All you need are some socks to make this adorable mermaid stuffed animal.

It's easy to make your own stuffed animals sometimes. I usually store old clothes for reuse after making dolls or clothes for dolls, so I always have a big bag of fabric cutouts or unpaired socks. I looked in my bag and found 2 fluffy socks that will be perfect for making an adorable mermaid cat plush. Let's get started!

Difficulty: medium
Time needed: approximately 2 hours.

Supplies:

✳ 2 fluffy socks in different colors
✳ Cushion filling
✳ Yarn, needle, and scissors
✳ Blue, purple, and fuchsia felt fabric
✳ Black foam paper
✳ Liquid silicone glue
✳ Marker pen

Instructions:

This type of sock is very soft and has a fluffy texture similar to stuffed animals already. It is very easy to make dolls, since the seams are completely hidden, plus you don't have to be an expert in sewing to make it look great.

The size of this doll will depend on the size of the socks, so if you want your mermaid cat to be very large, you can choose a larger sock size. Try to choose a solid color to make the cat body and a vivid or patterned color to make the mermaid tail. You can use any color of thread because it will not be seen at all.

Thread your needle to begin sewing, and consider doubling your thread so that the seams are more resistant.

Simply sew along the lines you drew, don't worry if you are not an expert in sewing, the seams will be completely hidden.

Then, cut the excess cloth on the outside of your sewn seams, and flip the socks rightways again. Repeat this process to make both the body of the cat and also the mermaid tail.

Turn the socks inside out and place them so that the heel part is on the front and facing up.

In the following image I have marked the lines that will serve as a guide for sewing and cutting—be careful! Note that the black lines are where you should sew, and the red lines are where you should cut.

I suggest you draw the lines before cutting.

Take a good amount of cushion stuffing and fill the cat sock, making sure to push padding inside the ears. Fill up to the heel area of the sock, then cut the excess fabric.

Now take the needle and thread again, and join the 2 pieces, making a seam around the top edge of the tail.

The next step will be to insert the cat sock you just filled inside the tail of the mermaid. If you prefer, add a little cushion filling into the fin area to fill them out, then insert the body inside of the cat. The tail should be situated around the waist.

This stuffed animal is almost finished! Now we will just add our details.

Look at the following image to see how I cut some details out of felt to decorate the stuffed animal: a scale-shaped purple belt and some felt cuts in blue that will be the lines of the head and the back of the cat.

To make eyes, mouth, and whiskers, I decided to use black foam paper to provide different textures.

And with the piece of gray sock left over I made 2 circles that will be the front legs of the cat.

To make the paws of the cat, we have to make some sort of fabric circle. Take 1 of the circles of gray cloth and stitch around the contour a simple seam, when you reach the point where you started to sew, pull the thread to gather the cloth but do not cut it, the cloth ball will form. Then fill it with padding and give 4 or 5 stitches to close the hole where you filled.

Do the same with the other cloth circle to form the other leg.

Join the paws to the gray body, just above the mermaid tail. Make several stitches so that it is secure. Make sure you leave a small gap between the paws to add something between his hands.

Use liquid silicone glue to stick the rest of the pieces in place. Use only a small amount of this glue so it doesn't seep out. Wait for it to dry, around 2 hours.

Don't forget to add the lines of the area of the back and you can also make a small felt star or place a small object that you have at home, and adhere this also with liquid silicone glue.

Did you imagine that you could make a stuffed animal yourself by reusing some socks? What an adorable stuffed animal, Meow!

Mermaid Lantern

Take the light of the mermaids wherever you go.

This time I will show you how to transform a glass jar into a mermaid lantern.

Making this craft requires very few materials and you will be able to take it to any dark place as if it were a flashlight. It also occurs to me that it can be a great handmade gift, for that person you know loves the mermaids. Let's do it!

Difficulty: easy
Time required: 30 minutes of work + drying time.

Supplies:

- ⭐ Glass jar
- ⭐ Masking tape
- ⭐ Mermaid silhouettes
- ⭐ Tissue paper, parchment paper, or another traceable paper
- ⭐ Acrylic paints (I used DecoArt Americana in: Crystal Glitter Gloss Enamels Turquoise DAGG10-30, Ice Crystal DGD09-30)
- ⭐ Sponge
- ⭐ White glue
- ⭐ Scissors
- ⭐ Garland of lights

Instructions:

You can use any type of recycled jar for this project, and give it whole new life!

We begin by placing masking tape around the outline of the glass bottle, about a quarter of the way up the jar. This will help you paint perfectly straight, which will give our craft a very professional look.

Then take the glitter paint and apply a layer throughout the bottom of the jar with the help of a sponge. I recommend that you blot the paint in small touches because if you drag the sponge, the paint will not stick to the glass properly.

The jar that I used also has a glass lid, so I painted that as well. Then it must be left to dry completely, to subsequently apply a second coat of paint.

It took my paint around 6 hours to dry. Once yours is dry, remove the masking tape. Admire how perfectly straight your painting is!

It's time to paste the silhouettes of mermaid, seaweed, and marine animals. You can trace them from the template on page 166 and transfer to thicker paper, then cut them out and color both sides of the paper with permanent black marker, this way they will be black on both sides.

To stick it to the jar, I used white glue because when it dries it becomes transparent, making it ideal for this glass jar. You must paste the silhouettes on the inside of the jar.

Finally, we will apply a layer of transparent glitter paint all over the jar and let it dry completely before introducing the garland lights. This layer of paint will give you a beautiful, shiny effect. When it has dried, you can add a garland of lights inside and your mermaid lantern will be ready to use.

What an incredible effect—it seems as though there is a small mermaid inside the glass jar.

Mermaid Slime

Sure, you've heard of the popular science project slime; people make it into all different themes, with different colors and textures, the options are endless!

But I bet you haven't seen this one before—we are making a simple mermaid slime inspired by the ocean. If you're ready for fun, gather all the ingredients and let's get started.

Difficulty: easy
Time needed: 5 minutes of preparation and many hours of fun.

Supplies:

- ✳ 250g of transparent school glue
- ✳ Blue powder glitter
- ✳ 1 tablespoon baking soda
- ✳ Saline solution for cleaning contact lenses
- ✳ Plastic marine animals
- ✳ 1 clear jar
- ✳ 1 big bowl
- ✳ A spoon to mix

Instructions:

Use a large bowl to make this mixture. Pour your transparent school glue into the bowl.

Now add a good amount of blue glitter, and mix to combine the 2 ingredients.

Add a tablespoon of baking soda to the mixture and stir with the spoon for at least 30 seconds so that the baking soda dissolves.

And now the most important ingredient, the contact lens solution which will cause this viscous liquid to become slime. However, before buying this product, read the label and make sure that its composition contains boric acid, which will be the key component to make the slime.

There are no exact amounts here, you should start with just a spoonful of the liquid solution and combing this with everything in your bowl. If it is not enough, add another spoonful and keep stirring. You can add as many spoonfuls as necessary so that the slime is formed, being sure to mix between each addition.

Once the mixture is no longer sticking to the bowl, it's time to mix it with your hands.

Then you can enjoy your slime!

Store your slime inside a transparent jar for safekeeping.

This jar is also a very nice decoration to decorate the shelf of your room

Give it a marine touch by adding some sea creatures. You can add plastic animals or you can make your own with polymer clay, like the ones in the photo. I've shown you some projects with that material, so you can refer to those if you want to create your own marine animals.

This mermaid slime is like having the sea inside a jar!

Mermaid Miniature School Supplies

You can make mermaid school supplies for your dolls!

People used to say, "when you get older you will stop playing with dolls." 😊 Okay, I don't play with them like before, but I still like to make clothes and accessories.

In this project, I will show you how to make a small backpack, a notebook, and a pencil case all inspired by the world of mermaids. What else can you make?

Difficulty: medium
Time needed: About 2 hours, more or less.

Supplies:

★ Glitter foam paper blue and pink colors
★ Tissue paper, parchment paper, or another traceable paper
★ A zipper of 20cm
★ Liquid silicone glue
★ Superglue
★ Chopsticks
★ Colored markers
★ Glitter cardboard
★ A sheet of bond paper
★ Scissors
★ Pencil

Instructions:

With a pencil, trace the templates on page 167 onto parchment paper.

Transfer the templates to the glitter foam paper—do this on the side that does not have glitter.

First, place the parchment paper on the foam paper, so that it is in contact with the graphite of the pencil, then press on the pencil area with some rounded object (like the back of the scissors). The pencil marks will be fixed to the foam paper.

Then cut out all the pieces in the corresponding colors.

Also using liquid silicone glue, join this piece of zipper with 1 of the backpack pieces, paste it across the edge using very little amount of glue. Look at the following image to see how to do this.

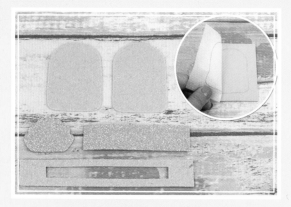

Take the piece that has a rectangle cut in its interior and, on the side that does not have glitter, glue the zipper. Place the zipper in such a way that the zipper falls inside the glitter area. Adhere this with liquid silicone glue.

Then let it dry and then trim any excess fabric from the zipper.

Now take the other backpack piece and glue it to the other edge. Make sure you stick it so that the glitter area is visible on the outside.

Add the pink rectangular piece of foam paper, to be the base of the backpack. Using the liquid silicone glue, glue it in the lower area starting just below the zipper.

Let it dry.

The next piece that we must place is the pocket in the shape of a shell.

Glue it to the front of the backpack, but in this case, put glue on the bottom edge of the pocket only. We want this piece to look like it forms a small bag to store things, as if it were a real backpack.

Cut 2 thin strips of pink glitter foam approximately 5mm thick. These will be the straps of the backpack. Make a few small cuts on the back of the backpack, to insert the strips, and stick them inside with liquid silicone glue. Also put a small strip on the top, which will be the handle of the backpack.

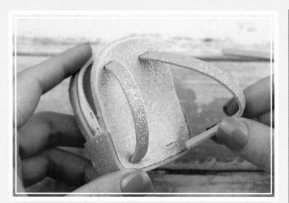

Making the pencil case is very easy. Cut out the pieces in the shape of a mermaid tail in a blue paper glitter foam and use pink for the small pieces that form the scales on the upper part of the case.

Join the pieces with superglue, because very little quantity is enough and when dealing with such small pieces, it is better to use a glue that does not stick out at the edges, thus the final result will be cleaner.

Put glue on the side edges only, leaving the top free to put pencils in.

As an ornament, stick on the outside the pieces of pink foam paper.

The small backpack is finished and we can move on to the rest of the supplies.

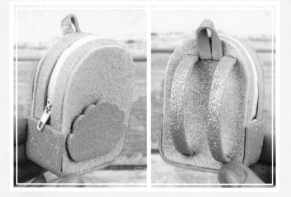

We are going to make some mini crayons. We will need round wooden toothpicks.

Use markers of various colors to make these pencils. Paint 1 of the tips of the toothpick, leave a small area unpainted just below, and then continue painting to create the mini pencil.

Then cut the stick of a similar size to the hollow of the case to be able to put them inside.

Make several pencils of different colors.

Hasn't this little pencil case been easy? Let's move on to the notebook.

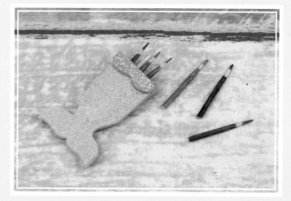

Cut the shape for the cover of the notebook in glitter cardboard, and cut several sheets of paper to make the inside pages.

Make small folds in the piece of cardboard to form the spine of the notebook.

Put all the inner sheets together and stick them to the back of the notebook on the inside. Use liquid silicone glue to stick this and let it dry at least 2 hours.

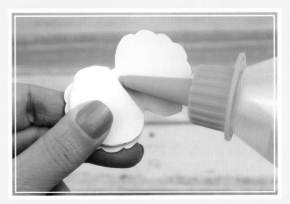

Decorate the outside of the notebook with the other piece of the template cut out in pink glitter foam paper.

Now your dolls are all ready for mermaid school with these miniature tools. 😎

MERMAID TAIL LIGHT

Make your own illuminated decoration in the shape of a mermaid tail.

I have always been impressed by big luminous signs, I love those big ones with light bulbs like those in Las Vegas! So now we will create our own with light bulbs in the shape of a mermaid tail. Are you ready?

Difficulty: difficult
Time required: around 3 hours of work + drying time.

Supplies:

- ✳ Pressed gray cardboard of 3mm
- ✳ A sheet of bond paper
- ✳ Carbon paper
- ✳ White glue
- ✳ Masking tape
- ✳ Acrylic paints (I used DecoArt Americana in: Snow White DA01, Americana Crystal Glitter Gloss Enamels Pink DAGG09-30 and Turquoise DAGG10-30)
- ✳ Water
- ✳ Awl
- ✳ Scissors, cutter
- ✳ Pencil
- ✳ Sponge to paint
- ✳ Garland of led lights that work with batteries

Instructions:

On a sheet of paper, draw the shape of a mermaid tail, making sure that the base is a straight line so that it remains standing. You can look at the mermaid tail that I have drawn to make yours.

You could draw directly on the cardboard, but I recommend making the template on paper because you can erase and practice as many times as you need.

Then use carbon paper to transfer the drawing on a sheet of pressed cardboard of 3mm.

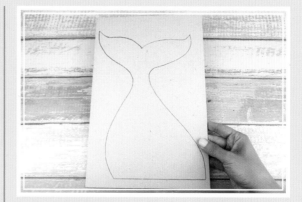

Now that you have your design on the cardboard, cut it out. This type of cardboard is very thick, so it is difficult to trim it with a pair of scissors—you will probably need to use a cutter. If you are small, it is better that you ask an adult to help with this step.

We will make the holes where the light bulbs will go. First draw with pencil the points where you want to have light bulbs, leaving a space of approximately 1cm around all edges.

Keep in mind that you should only make as many holes as light bulbs your garland has. So count the light bulbs and divide the points proportionally so that they have the same distance between them.

Then make the holes with a hole-puncher, the size of the holes should be large enough to fit the bulbs securely.

To make the outline of our light we must make strips of cardboard 3cm wide. These strips should cover the entire perimeter of the mermaid tail, so make long strips, then you can cut the excess.

Look at the following image, I have drawn a line with pencil on each cardboard strip. That line is at a distance of 1cm from the edge. This line will serve as a guide for pasting by the edge of the mermaid tail.

In the picture you also see a glass with water and a sponge since we must moisten the cardboard to be able to mold it, go to the next step to see how.

This type of cardboard is very rigid, so it is necessary to moisten it to bend it.

Since our mermaid tail has many curved shapes, we need to moisten the cardboard strips so that they adapt to these shapes. Just a small amount of water should be enough, so remove any excess water from the sponge before putting it on the cardboard.

There's no need to moisten the strip of cardboard that will be the base since it will be straight.

Now place the mermaid tail on the table and mold the cardboard strip following the contour. Cut the excess cardboard with scissors when wet, so that it cuts very easily.

It should remain in that position until it dries and that way the cardboard will take the curved shape permanently. You can add masking tape so that it stays fixed while it dries.

Once you have completely dried, you can now stick the strips to the mermaid tail using white glue. Remember that we draw a line 1cm from the margin, it is on that line where you have to paste the outline of the mermaid tail.

When it is dry, apply glitter paint—I am using pink and blue colors and apply it with a sponge to blur the transition zone between each color. Let the paint dry completely before moving on to the next step.

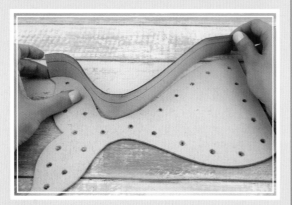

Cool! The hardest part is already done.

Now our craft is nearly done, but the gray color of the cardboard is not too pretty.

Apply a layer of white acrylic paint all over, and let it dry.

Finally put each bulb in a hole, leaving the cable in the back so it is not visible.

To make it easier to place the light bulbs, you can tape the cable to the back, or you can also use the instant drying glue or hot gun glue.

And our illuminated mermaid tail is already finished! It is a beautiful ornament to place it on your bedside table. 😍

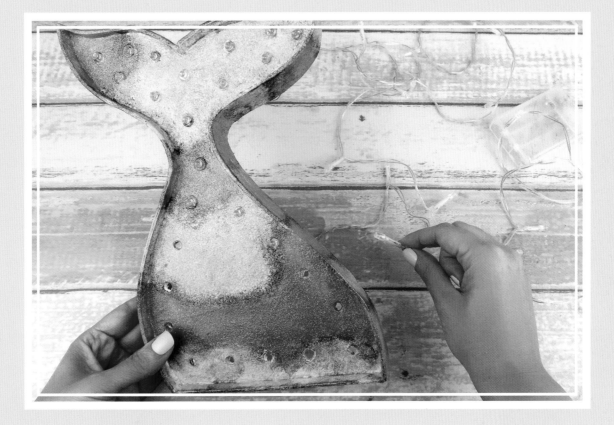

Mermaid Shoes

Customize your shoes with unique mermaid scales.

Why have regular old shoes if you can turn them into something so beautiful? These sneakers are inspired by mermaid tails, with their bright, metallic scales!

Difficulty: easy
Time required: around 2 hours of work + drying time.

Supplies:

* 1 pair light-colored cloth shoes (if you have some old ones at home, this is a great way to give them new life!)
* Masking tape
* Acrylic paints (I used DecoArt Americana in: True Blue DAO36-3, Black DAO67-3, Sapphire DPM17-30, Aquamarine DPM16-30, Glitter Celebration Pink DGD10-30)
* Fabric Painting Medium DAS10-3
* Tissue paper, parchment paper, or another traceable paper
* A small piece of cereal box cardboard
* Pencil
* Scissors
* Paintbrush

Instructions:

Remove the shoelaces and set them aside so they don't get dirty.

Use masking tape to protect the rubber soles and the toe of the shoes. If yours have some detail that you do not want to be stained with paint, cover it with masking tape too.

In the following figure you will see a scale shape. Trace it and transfer it into cereal box cardboard. We will only need 1 scale to paint all of them on both shoes.

Use the cardboard scale as a template and draw it on the shoe repeatedly to form the mermaid scale skin pattern.

Start drawing from the back of the shoe toward the toe. Make horizontal rows of scales, and then begin again in the bottom row, and so on, until the shoes are completely covered on both sides.

Notice that I haven't added scales to the shoelace eyelet area; this is because we'll paint that a solid color.

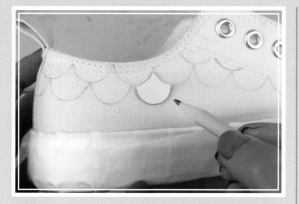

It's time to add color. To transform normal paint into fabric paint, we must mix it with fabric painting medium, which is a product that will make the paint more elastic and suitable for washing. By mixing this product with paint, you can decorate any cloth item. Follow the manufacturer's instructions to obtain the correct proportions of the mixture.

Use a fine brush to fill all the scales—I used metallic blue paint to get the true illusion of scales. Add some pink or turquoise scales too, to create some contrasts.

For the outline of the scales we will use black paint. It is easier to draw these lines with a very fine brush. Remember that you must also mix the black paint with the fabric painting medium.

For the area of the eyelets I have chosen a non-metallic regular blue color, which will make the metallic color of the scales stand out more.

Wait until the shoes are dry and then remove the masking tape that protected the rubber areas you didn't paint.

If the paint has stained any area of the sole, try to remove it with a damp cotton swab.

Finally, put back the laces and now you can show off your new mermaid shoes! They will be the most original shoes in your school.

This time I'm glad I don't have a mermaid tail, so I can use my new custom shoes. 😎

Mermaid Shelf

Organize your area with this adorable mermaid-shaped shelf.

In this chapter I will show you how to make a small bookcase to organize your desk or craft area, and of course, if you weren't sure, it will be a mermaid bookcase. Besides being a useful handicraft, it is also an object that will decorate your room.

Difficulty: medium
Time required: approximately 3 hours.

Supplies:

- ✭ Cardboard
- ✭ Carbon paper
- ✭ Colored foam paper in pink, white, blue, green, yellow, light beige, brown, gray, and lilac
- ✭ Liquid silicone glue
- ✭ Acrylic paints (I used DecoArt Americana in: Dark Chocolate DAO65-3, Lamp (Ebony) Black DAO67-3, Snow White DA01, Shoreline DA365-3, Baby Pink DAO31-3, Grey Sky DA111-3, Peaches 'n Cream DAO23-3)
- ✭ Pink blusher
- ✭ Bright plastic adhesive
- ✭ Pencil, scissors, and paintbrush

Instructions:

For this craft, there is template on page 168—however, this template is not full size since the drawing must measure 25cm high. You can ask an adult to help you expand the image to the correct size and trace it, or you can find the full-size template on my website www.elmundodeisa.com

Now that you have the template, it is time to transfer the drawing to the cardboard, but it will only be necessary to paint the outer contour of the template on the cardboard. Use carbon paper to transfer the drawing to 2 separate pieces of cardboard.

Then cut them out.

Cut out this same shape in both pink and white foam paper (2 each) and stick these to the cardboard, 1 color on each side of the cardboard.

This padded cardboard will be the 2 sides of the shelf—I made sure pink was on the inside, and white was on the outside (since it will be covered).

As you can see in the following image, I have also stuck some strips of pink glitter foam paper all around the cardboard to cover the edges.

Cut out each part of the mermaid drawing in foam paper of the colors you see in the image. A trick to pass the template to foam paper is to trace the drawing on parchment paper and then place this paper on the foam paper, so that the pencil graphite is in contact with the foam paper, then press on the drawing and it will be transferred to the foam paper. This will be the easiest way to obtain all the pieces that make up the mermaid drawing.

Then form your mermaid, looking at the template for guidance to see which pieces go further back in the figure.

Look at the picture of the shelf already finished, you can see that some pieces overlap a little. For example, the part that goes back is the largest part of the hair in brown, on top of this piece you can stick the body, then paste the face overlapping on the body the area of the neck and above the face, then add the part of the hair that corresponds to the fringe. The template will guide you the whole way to know where to place each piece.

You can use a small amount of silicone liquid glue to paste these pieces of foam paper.

Once your mermaid is put together, use a fine brush and acrylic paints to give the face some color. You can also add some details with paintings in other parts of the mermaid, such as some lines in the hair, draw the fingers of the hand, and some white scales on the tail.

To give depth effect, I like to apply a little paint on the edges of the foam paper with a small sponge. First drain the excess paint from the sponge on an absorbent paper towel and then dab the entire edge—I always use paint colors that are similar to the foam paper that I want to shade, this gives a more professional finish (in the list of materials you can see the colors that I have used).

Once the figure of the mermaid is finished, it is time to stick it on 1 of the sides of the shelf. Glue it on the part that is white—the mermaid is made to be a little smaller than the white outline, you will see a white border around it that will make the colors stand out more.

So far we have completed the 2 side pieces of our shelf, now we will make the shelves themselves.

Now I will show you how to make a shelf, but remember—you will need 2 of them!

Cut 3 pieces of cardboard. 2 of them must be equally sized at 20cm × 2cm, and also cut a larger piece that must measure 20cm × 9cm. These 3 pieces of cardboard will form a shelf.

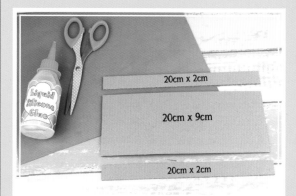

I have chosen to make my shelves lilac color, so I used foam paper to line the 3 pieces of cardboard, and pasted it with liquid silicone glue.

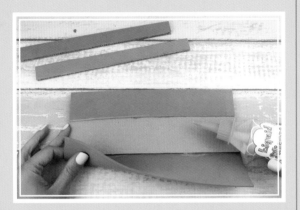

Use the liquid silicone glue to adhere the 2 smaller pieces to the larger one to form the shelf. Look at the following image to see how to do it. Repeat this process to make your second shelf.

By now, we have finished all the pieces that make up the shelf.

They are 2 shelves and 2 lateral sides. So all we have to do is connect them with the liquid silicone glue.

Leave a gap between the shelves tall enough to fit all the things you want to keep here.

Thanks to this beautiful mermaid shelf, you can keep everything in perfect order

Fake Mermaid Milkshake

It may look like a shake, but really it's a secret hiding place! 🙂

Whenever I go to an ice cream parlor, I ask for the most overloaded milkshake that has everything. Some places even sell mermaid shakes, can you believe it? They have delicious chocolate mermaid tails and ice cream in blue, turquoise, pink, lilac—wow! I just had to make a craft inspired by these shakes.

But below, there's a secret place to store things inside the mermaid milkshake.

Difficulty: medium
Time required: around 3 hours of work + drying time.

Supplies:

- ⭐ 1 glass jar
- ⭐ Jumping Clay in white, blue, pink, brown, lilac colors
- ⭐ 1 Porex sphere of approx. 8cm in diameter
- ⭐ Small colored Porex balls
- ⭐ A plastic drinking straw
- ⭐ Liquid silicone glue
- ⭐ Colored foam paper: brown and white
- ⭐ White glue
- ⭐ White powder glitter
- ⭐ Colored markers
- ⭐ Wooden sticks for crafts
- ⭐ Acrylic paints (I used DecoArt Americana in: Snow White DA01; Metallic or Glitter paint: Americana Gloss Enamels Royal Fuchsia DAG151-30 and Turquoise DAGT10-30)
- ⭐ Scissors, pencil, and paintbrush

Instructions:

For the glass jar, you can simply recycle a jar of preserves—choose an appropriate size to keep your secret items inside. Ideally, the size resembles that of a smoothie or milkshake.

To make it look like the jar is full of milkshake, we must paint the inside. Choose colors that look like a real milkshake! In my case I'm going to simulate a raspberry shake with blueberry syrup, so I chose fuchsia and turquoise colors.

We will use paint suitable for glass (check the list of materials to see what I have used). Make some lines on the inside of the glass jar with 1 of your colors to look like syrup dripping down. Put a couple layers so it looks thick enough and no longer transparent. If necessary, apply several layers, allowing to dry between each.

Once the syrup lines have dried, it is time to add your next color, which is your ice cream. Pour a large amount of paint inside the jar and turn it slowly so that the paint spreads all over the glass.

The glass of the inner part of the jar must be completely covered by paint. Let this dry and if necessary, apply another coat of paint later.

Take a Porex sphere and cut it in half. Mine measures 8cm in diameter, but the size will depend on the lid of your glass jar. You must choose a size that suits the jar lid.

Glue this half sphere on the lid of the jar, using liquid silicone glue to paste it. Let it dry before moving on to the next step.

To make the chocolate that overflows the jar, we will use brown paper foam. Cut a strip as long as the outline of the jar. Draw the chocolate drops with a pencil and cut this shape with the scissors. Then glue it to the contour of the lid.

Next is the mermaid style ice cream ball. So, we need Jumping Clay of pink and blue colors. Put a chunk of these 2 colors on your foam sphere—remember, this clay sticks to its surface and needs several hours to dry, so it is not necessary to use glue here. Cover the entire half sphere with your ice cream colors and make some pinches with your fingers to give it a more realistic texture.

Any shake worth its salt must have many sweet complements and extras, so, with Jumping Clay, we will create mini donuts that will be added on the drinking straw.

First, make a small brown ball of about 1 inch, this ball will be the donut. Make a second ball of another color about ¼-inch, this small ball will be the icing.

Slightly press the brown ball with the palm of your hand and make a hole in the middle using a drinking straw.

To make the frosting, press down the small ball and also make a hole in the center. Give a little bit of shape to the edges to make it look more realistic.

Then place the frosting on the donut and put some lines of white paint on top.

Make 5 or 6 mini donuts with various colors of glaze and let them dry for a few hours. The idea is to use colors that remind us of mermaids.

When all the donuts are dry, insert a drinking straw through them and then stick the straw into the Porex ball that we decorated as ice cream in the previous step.

I used a silicone mold to create more fake candies, like a mermaid tail with Jumping Clay.

This is a simple kitchen mold, however the type of modeling paste that we are using is non-toxic, so you can use it for this craft and just be sure to wash the mold before using it for food again. Fill the mold with Jumping Clay and let it dry, then unmold to get your mermaid tail.

If you do not have a mold, you can make the mermaid tail with your hands (look at some of the other crafts in this book).

I am getting hungry! 😋

The next sweet will be colorful marshmallows—they almost look like clouds. Take Jumping Clay of white, pink, blue, and lilac colors and roll out small logs of each color.

Join the 4 colors and take each end with one hand, now carefully turn the clay with one hand in each direction. Let this dry, and then cut it into pieces with scissors to create these very realistic marshmallows. You can now stick them on the ice cream ball that we created before.

Then we will make a sweet that I love, sour candy strips! They are delicious, and where I live, we call this unicorn bacon.

To make this bacon we will use white foam paper—cut a strip 3cm thick and 15cm long. Draw colored lines along this strip with markers and let the ink dry.

Once dry, mix a little white glue with white powder glitter. Now with a brush apply a thin layer of this mixture onto the strip of foam paper.

When dry, gently bend this into a g-zag shape and insert a wooden stick through each. Stick this onto the ice cream ball we've created.

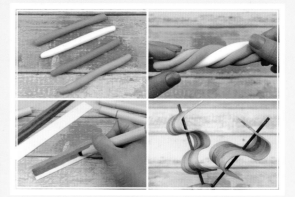

To continue decorating, you can also make some waffles rolled with brown foam paper and place small Porex balls of many colors throughout the ice cream to look like sprinkles.

All you have to do is unscrew the lid in order to hide all your things hide inside. What an original idea!

This looks just like a real mermaid milkshake, nobody will know it's really a secret jar!

Mermaid House Lamp

A mermaid house that will light up your dreams!

If I think of where the mermaids live, I imagine a city at the bottom of the sea, with many houses shaped like shells, and I imagine their windows are illuminated at night.

This inspired me to make a conch lamp, and it's a great idea to have a small light spot in your room when it's time to sleep.

Difficulty: medium
Time required: around 3 hours of work + drying time.

Supplies:

* ⋆ 1 balloon
* ⋆ Aluminum foil
* ⋆ 1kg modeling paste, air drying
* ⋆ Hot glue
* ⋆ Acrylic paints (I used DecoArt Americana in: Baby Pink DAG31, Lilac Meadow DA367, Peony Pink DA215, Sour Apple DA275, Desert Turquoise DA044, Ocean Blue DA270, Bright Yellow DA227, Snow White DA01, Peacock Pearl DA314)
* ⋆ Gloss Varnish DuraClear DecoArt Americana DS19
* ⋆ Water
* ⋆ Modeling tools
* ⋆ Awl
* ⋆ Scissors
* ⋆ Paintbrush
* ⋆ Garland lights

Instructions:

To make this craft, we'll have to get our hands a little dirty!

Start by blowing up a balloon to the size you want your light to be, but keep in mind that it should not be too inflated so it does not explode when working on it.

To make it easier to work with the balloon, place it on some object to serve as a base. I used a roll of masking tape, or a cup will also work.

With your hands or with the help of a modeling tool, cover the whole balloon with clay—put a generous layer so the lamp will be resistant.

As it is an oval shape, you must first cover one part, let it dry, and then turn it over and cover the other part. But don't cover the balloon mouthpiece with clay, because when it is completely dry, you must remove the balloon and it will be easier if the mouthpiece sticks out.

To move on to the next step, the modeling paste must be completely dry, so it is best to let it dry all night and keep working tomorrow.

Now that have dried enough hours, it is time to remove the balloon. Hold onto the mouthpiece sticking out, and carefully pop it, then pull out the plastic.

You also have to make an opening in the widest part—this hole has to be big enough so later you can put a garland of lights into it. You can use scissors to make this hole. It's time to express your creativity!

With aluminum foil, we are going to turn this balloon into a conch shape, so roll up pieces of aluminum foil and mold them into different shapes to create your mermaid house. Use hot glue to attach the foil. See how I created my conch, this can inspire you to create yours.

Once dry, cover the aluminum foil with clay and smooth it with your fingers or with a modeling tool.

The clay is easier to spread when it's a bit moist, so if you need to you can spray a bit of water to keep it malleable.

If you need to create more shapes with the foil on the clay, wait until it is completely dry before continuing.

To paint, we will use acrylics (see the list above if you want to know what colors I used).

I like to paint a first layer with the paint diluted in water, so I get a lighter base, and then create shadows and accentuate areas with undiluted paint.

When the paint has dried, I recommend you apply 2 layers of varnish to protect the paint, and then you can also clean the lamp with a wet cloth when it gets dirty. Let it dry between each layer.

The mermaid house is almost ready!

Remember that our goal is to turn it into a lamp, so we will have to make holes to let the light to come out. Help yourself with a pointed tool to create the holes (an awl served me well). First I drew the shapes of the holes with a pencil, and then I repeatedly poked through with the awl until I got rid of the clay.

Make as many holes as you want.

To finish, place a garland of lights inside this mermaid house and your lamp will be ready to use.

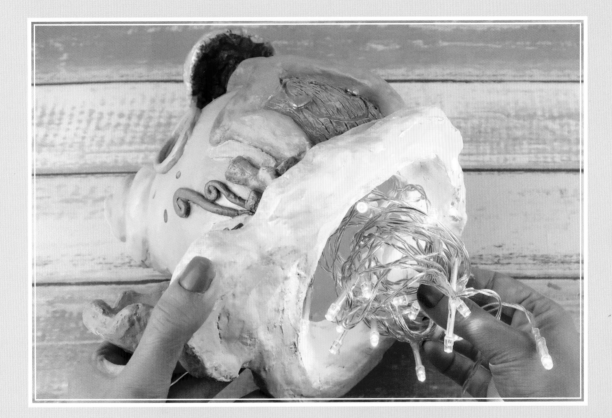

Besides being a very fun craft, now my bedside
table looks cuter than ever. 😊

Mermaid phone case

Decorate your smartphone in mermaid style!

One of my hobbies is collecting phone cases, so I like to create my own and switch them out often. I confess, when I take a selfie in the mirror I like the phone case to look pretty. ☺

Difficulty: medium
Time needed: about 2 hours + the drying time.

Supplies:

- ⭒ Simple mobile phone case
- ⭒ Lilac polymer clay
- ⭒ White glue
- ⭒ Superglue or liquid silicone glue
- ⭒ Bright rhinestones, sequins, pearls, or any bright ornament that you like
- ⭒ Parchment paper
- ⭒ Pink glitter
- ⭒ Gloss Varnish DuraClear DecoArt Americana DS19
- ⭒ DecoArt Metallic Lustre Silver Spark ML03C-28
- ⭒ Paintbrush

Instructions:

We will start by making the central figure of our mobile phone case, the polymer clay mermaid tail. This kind of modeling clay requires drying in the oven, so if you are small it is better to ask an adult for help with this step.

First, we will make 2 small balls of lilac polymer clay, the largest one should measure about 1 inch and the small one will be ¼-inch.

Take the biggest ball and make a cone shape (follow my example).

With the palm of your hand, flatten it and shape it with your fingers to resemble a mermaid tail.

With the small ball, make a pressed triangle shape and join both pieces as shown in the image, run your finger over so they are seamlessly connected.

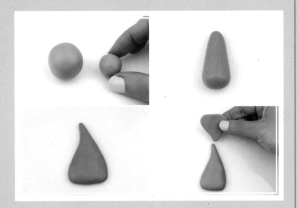

Use a sharp-edged modeling tool to cut out a bit of the small triangle you joined and to form the fins.

To create the scales, we will need a plastic drinking straw. With a pair of scissors, cut a small chunk out of 1 end to create an arch or half-moon shape on 1 side. Now create the scales by lightly pressing the straw along the entire mermaid tail.

Also make some lines in the fin area to give a more realistic texture.

To give it a more glamorous look, you can apply a product that I love called Metallic Lustre; it gives you spectacular silver shimmer (see the materials list if you want to know what kind I used).

Perfect! The mermaid tail is now ready, and it is time to bake so that it hardens. Put your figure on a parchment paper–lined baking sheet so that it doesn't stick.

Follow the instructions given by the manufacturer of your polymer clay for baking. In my case, I needed to bake for 30 minutes at 230°F. Get an adult to help you with the oven.

When the 30 minutes have passed, let it cool completely.

It's time to decorate the case, and we have everything you need to customize it in the style of mermaids. I will use sequins that remind me of the scales, and also glitter, and adhesive rhinestones. If you feel like it, you can also use plastic beads or any bright ornament that you like.

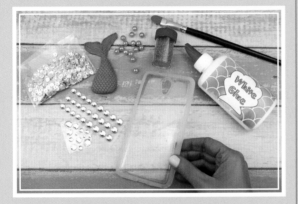

We will cover the whole case with pink glitter (or any color you like)—this will give a spectacular look.

Apply a generous layer of white glue all over the outside of the case. Do not worry about it being white, when it dries it will be completely transparent.

Carefully sprinkle the glitter over the glue before it dries. You must put a generous amount of glitter to cover the entire outside of the case. Then let it dry completely, this may take a few hours.

When the glue has dried, you can continue with the next step.

Using liquid silicone glue or superglue, stick the mermaid tail you made earlier onto the case.

To prevent the glitter from coming off when handling your phone, I recommend that you apply a layer of varnish on top of the glitter and also on the mermaid tail—this will also give a very nice bright touch.

Let the varnish dry before moving on to the next step.

Finally comes the most fun of this craft. Stick on all the sequins and decorations you want, the more the better.

To paste all this, use superglue or liquid silicone glue, but if you choose the silicone glue, use only a small amount for a cleaner result so the glue doesn't stick out .

Wow! This phone case came out so beautiful. I'm afraid I have a new favorite cover in my collection—I'm running to take a selfie. 😬

Mermaid Necklace

This mermaid necklace will be your new lucky charm.

I think you already know that I love mermaids—along with unicorns, they are the mythological beings that inspire me the most.

For this craft, I wanted something I could do with my own hands to give to my best friends, and I thought that a mermaid tail charm would be perfect. So, I got to work.

Difficulty: easy
Time required: about 1 hour of work + the drying time.

Supplies:

✳ Polymer clay of the colors that you prefer
✳ Tissue paper, parchment paper, or another traceable paper
✳ Wire for pendants
✳ Parchment paper
✳ Purpurin
✳ Glue for decoupage, DecoArt Americana DS106
✳ Gloss Varnish DuraClear DecoArt Americana DS19

Instructions:

Making this mermaid tail necklace is very easy, but since you have to use polymer clay that requires baking, ask an adult for help when it comes to handling the oven.

On page 169 you have a silhouette of a mermaid tail, this is the template to make your pendant, so you must trace it onto a piece of paper.

Now that you have your template ready, choose the color you prefer of polymer clay. Make an elongated drop shape and place it on the template to adjust to its shape. You can do it with your hands, or help yourself with a modeling tool.

I have decided to make the tail blue with fuchsia fins, I just love this color combination. You can see that the part of the fins is made in the same way as the part of the tail, just take polymer clay and adjust it to the shape of the template.

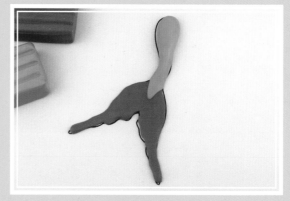

Now I'm going to give it some detail so that it looks more realistic and not so flat.

Roll out some polymer clay strands and place them around the border of the fin area, you can contrast the colors to make it more striking. I will also make some lines with a sharp object—it will look great with some texture!

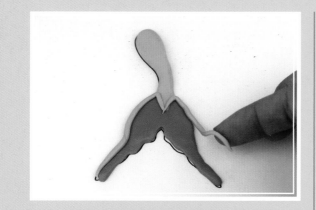

As it is a mermaid tail necklace, we need to add a wire to be able to hang it around the neck. I got the wires you see in the picture in a craft store, in the jewelry section.

With the help of a plier, make a rounded shape at the tip and then insert the wire into the top of the mermaid tail.

It is almost ready!

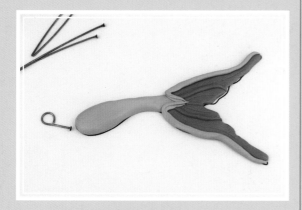

It's time to bake, so place your mermaid tail on a parchment paper–lined baking sheet to prevent it from sticking to the tray.

Follow the instructions indicated by the manufacturer of your polymer clay (I needed to bake mine for 30 minutes at 230°F).

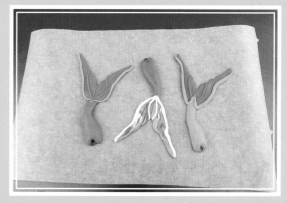

When the baking time has elapsed, allow it to cool completely before moving on to the next step.

It's time to shine our mermaid tail pendant. I have chosen glitter flakes because I think it is perfect to decorate this beautiful mermaid tail charm.

With a brush, place a thick layer of Decoupage DecoArt Americana DS106 glue, put glue only in the area where you want the glitter to stick.

Now sprinkle the glitter and it will stay stuck wherever you put the glue.

Then let it dry completely and finally apply a layer of Gloss Varnish DuraClear DecoArt American DS19 to protect the craft and have a shiny finish.

Now you will always be accompanied by the magic of the mermaids, because you bare a good luck charm made with your own hands!

MERMAID DECORATED LETTERS

Any corner of your house will be more fun if you decorate it with mermaid letters!

This craft is great for decorating a birthday party or any personalized celebration. I think customizing some papier-mâché letters will be a unique detail for any mermaid lover.

Difficulty: easy
Time required: about 1 hour of work + drying time.

Supplies:

* Cardboard or paper letters, you can find them in craft stores
* Acrylic paints (I used DecoArt Americana in: Teal Mint DA332-3, Royal Purple DA150-3, Lilac Meadow DA367-3, Peacock Teal DA326-3, and Royal Fuchsia DA151-3)
* Artificial flowers
* Adhesive rhinestone stickers
* Plastic beads
* Mermaid tail shapes or marine animals made with glitter foam paper (you can make them yourself or buy them in craft stores)
* Scissors
* Paintbrush
* Ruler
* Liquid silicone glue

Instructions:

This craft is all about decorating papier-mâché letters and therefore you can customize your own name or any word you like. These letters can be found in any craft store and there are many different sizes.

You will also need some mermaid-themed decorations. I have chosen plastic beads, adhesive rhinestones, artificial flowers, a mermaid tail, and seahorse figures that I made with glitter foam paper.

To begin, we will add color to the letters—in my case I have decided to decorate my name, "Isa." I have painted each letter with very different colors of acrylic paints to make a nice contrast (in the list of materials you can see the exact colors that I have used).

For the letter "I" I have chosen a nice mint color, the letter "S" will be purple and lilac, and the letter "A" will be turquoise and fuchsia. You can choose any colors you like!

When the paint has dried, it is time to decorate.

Let's start with the first letter. I have cut a mermaid tail shape in glitter foam paper—all you have to do is draw a mermaid tail shape and cut it with scissors, then paste it with liquid silicone glue.

I will also decorate by gluing many artificial flowers of pink, lilac, and fuchsia colors.

The next letter I will decorate with many plastic beads, this time I bought a very long fake pearl necklace, I separated them one by one and I glued them with liquid silicone glue. I also made a kind of algae with green paper glitter foam.

And since my name only has 3 letters, all we have left is the "A." If your name is longer, you can decorate other letters with other marine animals, or with many bright stickers, let your imagination run wild to create beautiful decorations.

For the last letter, I have pasted a seahorse shape that I made like the mermaid tail, with glitter foam paper.

And between the 2 different colors of the letter, I have placed some small bright plastic stickers. It is a simple decoration but very beautiful.

This craft has been quick and entertaining. It is easy to decorate this type of papier-mâché letters, you can make as many words as you want!

Bookmark Mermaid Friends

These little friends of the sea will accompany you in your reading hours.

This time we're going to sew, and I'll show you how to make some bookmarks for your books. Your new underwater friends will help you to always know by which page you left off.

These bookmarks are a little more difficult of a project, and if it is your first time sewing, it may not be so perfect—but with practice you will do it better every time, this is the beauty of learning.

Difficulty: difficult
Necessary time: 2 hours approximately.

Supplies:

✳ Felt fabric
✳ 1 sheet of paper
✳ Masking tape
✳ Silk paper
✳ Colored yarn similar to felt
✳ Pencil, scissors, and needle
✳ Tissue paper, parchment paper, or another traceable paper

Instructions:

Felt is a cloth made of wool, without knitting, which is made by pressing the wool. This makes the fabric so that when cut, it doesn't fray, so it is an ideal material for handicrafts, dolls, brooches, etc. You can also find synthetic felt or felt with a mixture of wool and synthetic material. All types of felt are acceptable to make this project, however I personally recommend using 100 percent wool felt, as it is much easier to sew and will also be kept in better condition over the years.

On page 170 you will find templates for the 3 marine animals—choose the one you like the most for your first bookmark. I have decided to start with the whale.

Trace the drawing on a sheet of paper. Notice in the following image that I have traced each of the parts of the drawing separately, because these will each need to be cut out of the felt fabric.

Cut out each piece of paper individually, stick the paper to the felt using masking tape. Now trim the paper and felt at the same time. Then discard the paper and . . .

Voilà! Your piece is ready.

Some pieces will need to be cut out more than once—the silhouette of the whale must be cut out twice in blue (without the water shooting out) and twice in green, which *should* include the jet of water. Using white felt, cut out 2 individual water jets, and also 2 blush dots in pink. Cut out 1 small piece of gray for the belly. Trace the eyes and the smile on a piece of tissue paper.

Let's start sewing. Take 1 of the pieces of blue felt and carefully tape the little face that you traced on top of it. This will serve as a guide to sew the eyes and smile. You must sew through the paper and the fabric at the same time—this type of paper is very thin and can then be removed easily. Another alternative is that you draw with a pencil directly on the felt, and then sew on top of the pencil, but if you choose this method, make sure that the pencil strokes are very soft so that they cannot be seen afterwards.

You should also sew on the pink blush dots and the gray belly; try to use thread colors similar to the felt you are sewing in each case.

To sew all this, you have to use a stitch called Back Stitch, which is ideal for embroidering contours, creating text, or drawing any shape or drawing. It involves making a simple stitch and going back to fill the gap and thus form a solid line. (See page 60 for Back Stitch instructions.)

Now that you have decorated the front of your blue whale, take the other blue piece and place it behind so they match up. We will join them using the stitch called Blanket Stitch, which is usually used to join 2 pieces by the edge of the cloth. A trick so that all the stitches are at the same distance is to draw some lines with a pen on your finger.

Next, I will explain how to make the Blanket Stitch (in the images I use a thread of different color to the felt so that you can see it more easily, but you should use the thread color indicated in the text):

1. Insert your thread carefully through the needle, and tie a knot at the end. Now place the 2 pieces of felt together and with the needle in the center of the 2 fabrics, go through the front fabric, the knot should be between the 2 fabrics.

2. Insert the needle from the front and through both fabrics at a time. Pull the thread but without tightening it, it should be loose in the front.
3. Now pass the needle by the thread that was loose and now you should pull a bit so it is tight.
4. Insert the needle back into the left side of the stitch you just made and repeat the process all the way around the fabric.

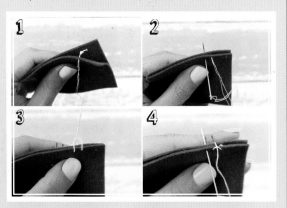

In the following image you can see how this stitch is applied to our whale.

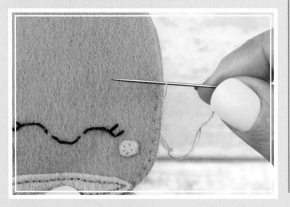

Before closing completely, sew together the 2 pieces of white felt that form the water jet, and place this between the 2 blue fabrics, in the highest part of the head—use the template to guide you since afterwards it must coincide with the other piece of felt. Then finish sewing to close.

Join the 2 pieces of plain color using the same type of stitch. Remember to use a thread that resembles the color of the felt.

At this point you have the silhouette of the whale in a plain color, and the front of the whale in blue. So let's join them.

Begin to join them from the lowest part, just where the fin ends at the bottom of the whale and take it from left to right. Use blue yarn and match the new stitches with the existing stitches.

Finish sewing at the curve of the head at the top.

Once the pieces are joined, you can use this in the pages of your book.

These bookmark animals are so adorable! Practice doing the crab and the jellyfish too, I am sure you will get better and better. 😍

TEMPLATES

Mermaid animal pens

There's a million fish in the sea, but I'm a mermaid

MERMAID HEADBAND

Mermaid felt doll

MERMAID SECRET DIARY

Mermaid miniature school supplies

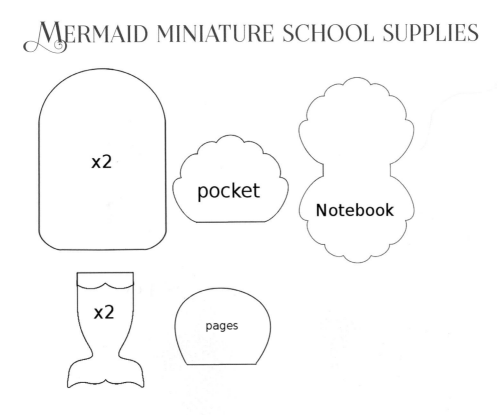

x2

pocket

Notebook

x2

pages

piece where the zipper will be glued
13.5cm x 2cm

base of the backpack
8.5cm x 2.4cm

MERMAID SHELF

MERMAID NECKLACE

BOOKMARK MERMAID FRIENDS

CONCLUSION

It has been quite an underwater adventure to create this book. I have put all my love into each project and page of this book, so I hope you enjoyed it as much as I have enjoyed creating it!

Remember that life is like the ocean, always full of adventures and challenges, but like the mermaids, each of us is a unique and fascinating being and there is nothing we can't achieve if we believe in ourselves and put our heart and soul into it.

Be creative, free, and passionate about any project you do throughout your life, and I am sure you will always succeed.

Thank you for immersing yourself in these pages and don't forget: Always be a mermaid!

With love, Isa ♡

ABOUT THE AUTHOR

Isabel Urbina Gallego lives in Madrid, Spain.

Isa has been always a creative person since she was a child—she used to spend her free time doing self-taught crafts. In 2014, she decided to turn this hobby into something professional, which is when she created her first YouTube channel called El Mundo de Isa, where she posts weekly videos in Spanish, her native language, on how to make creative crafts for both adults and children from scratch.

In 2016 El Mundo de Isa won Best Crafts Channel of the year by *Vlogger Prize*.

Since then, she has not stopped doing all kinds of step-by-step crafts, because it is what she is most passionate about.

Her community of fans soon grew, so she wanted to expand her horizons by creating a new channel on YouTube called Isa's World, where she explains her creations in English.

Isa is also the author of *Unicorn Crafts,* with multiple craft projects inspired by unicorns.

Isa loves to spend time with family, she is an animal lover, and her best moments are spent in the company of her 2 dogs, Arish and Noah, and with her professional and life partner, Víctor.

YouTube: www.youtube.com/mundodeisa and www.youtube.com/c/isasworld
Facebook: www.facebook.com/isalunahe
Instagram: www.instagram.com/isalunahe
Twitter: www.twitter.com/isalunahe
Blog: www.elmundodeisa.com